M000314935

THE STANDOUT EXPERIENCE

THE

STANDOUT

EXPERIENCE

HOW STUDENTS AND YOUNG PROFESSIONALS CAN RISE, SHINE, AND IMPACT WHEN IT MATTERS MOST

JOHN WALSH

LIONCREST
PUBLISHING

COPYRIGHT © 2020 JOHN WALSH
All rights reserved.

THE STANDOUT EXPERIENCE
How Students and Young Professionals Can Rise,
Shine, and Impact When It Matters Most

ISBN   978-1-5445-0743-9 *Hardcover*
       978-1-5445-0741-5 *Paperback*
       978-1-5445-0742-2 *Ebook*
       978-1-5445-0744-6 *Audiobook*

To everyone who wants to stand out, this book is written for you. I hope you rise to your highest potential, shine your leadership talent to help others, and impact the world to make it a better place. Go stand out—the world needs you!

CONTENTS

ACKNOWLEDGMENTS

My immense gratitude, admiration, and dedication go...

To my wife, Theresa: You have been a standout to me ever since we met. You make me a better person and you have always inspired, helped, and supported me. Without you, this would not be possible. Thank you for taking the journey together.

To Eva, Maddy Mae, and Grey: You have unlimited potential and you light up everyone's life around you. I can't wait to see who you become and what you will do to impact the world.

To Dad, Sharon, Mom, and Steve: I am who I am because of you. You have always loved me, supported me, and been a blessing in my life. There are simply not enough ways to say thank you.

To Chris and Anna: Through the good times and bad, we have always loved and supported each other. I want nothing more for you than to live your own standout life.

To Dave and Scott: Brothers to the end and family forever. I wouldn't change what we have for the world. You guys mean everything to me.

To my leaders, mentors, peers, friends, and those I've come to know: I have learned so much from you, and I hope I'm taking the best of you and paying it forward so other people can learn from your greatness.

To those I have hurt: I am sorry. You have taught me many valuable lessons about myself during and after our time together. I am a better person because of you, and I hope that is the greatest apology.

To Alex and everyone else at UF and UVA: To be the best, you have to learn from and work with the best. Thank you for your time, talents, resources, and investments in me. Go Gators! Go Hoos!

To David, Kacy, and the team at Scribe Media: Thank you for your patience, guidance, hard work, and incredible talent. Because you do what you do and care so much about the people you work with, you already stand out and this book isn't for you. David, your world-class support and the time you spent with me was going beyond standing out. I can't thank you enough.

INTRODUCTION

"The world accommodates you for fitting in, but it rewards you for standing out."

~MATSHONA DHLIWAYO

In many of life's biggest moments, only a few or worse, only one is chosen...

Admittance into America's colleges and universities, corporate job openings, and the dating scene are just a few examples in life where the odds are not in your favor.

Acceptance rates at many top colleges and universities are between 4 and 10 percent.[1] If attending college is on the horizon, your mission is to get accepted to your top choice and pick the *one* major, you think, will give you the best chance to fulfill all your hopes and dreams.

Maybe you're out of school and trying to survive in the ultra-competitive global marketplace, where an MBA is barely enough to get your foot in the interviewer's office door. In fact, with an average of over 250 resumes submitted for

---

1   *Top—100 Lowest Acceptance Rates,* www.USNews.com, https://www.usnews.com/best-colleges/rankings/lowest-acceptance-rate.

every corporate job opening, your chance of being the *one* candidate selected for each of those opportunities is less than one-half of a percent.[2]

What about love? If you subscribe to the notion that there is only *one* person among the billions of people on the planet who you are destined to be with—your soulmate—the odds of finding that special someone have been scientifically calculated at approximately .010 percent.[3]

Perhaps the most important fact among all this data is that you're only going to choose *one* life. On average, you will live roughly 29,000 days, making 35,000 conscious and unconscious choices per day.[4] Based on the accumulation of those choices, you could experience life in an infinite number of ways, but you will only live *one of them.*

These statistics validate the immensely competitive and highly variable nature of the world you're living in. They exemplify how challenging it is to emerge from the crowd of similarly qualified peers and become the *chosen one* in many of life's opportunities for achievement and happiness.

Adding fuel to this fire is the pressure to succeed coming from your parents, family, friends, and others. They're all pushing you to attend a great school, pick the perfect major, get the best job, perform at the highest level, raise

2   Peter Economy, *11 Interesting Hiring Statistics You Should Know,* www.Inc.com, May 5, 2015, https://www.inc.com/peter-economy/19-interesting-hiring-statistics-you-should-know.html.

3   Amy Chan, *Why the Myth of the Soulmate Is Still Holding Us Back,* www.verilymag.com, January 18, 2018, https://verilymag.com/2018/01/finding-your-soul-mate-meaning-what-is-a-soul-mate.

4   *Average life expectancy in North America for those born in 2019, by gender and region (in years),* www.Statista.com, https://www.statista.com/statistics/274513/life-expectancy-in-north-america/.

an amazing family, and meet any number of other societal expectations.

There is good news, however, because the solution to these problems is simple...

You need to learn how to stand out!

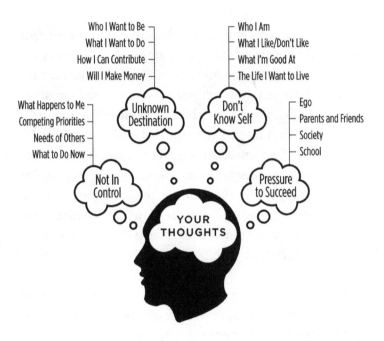

THE EVOLUTION OF STANDING OUT

You, and so many others, have incredible gifts and talents, but it might seem like you only scratch the surface of what you're truly capable of. Meanwhile, the world waits for the special few to step up and solve the many problems and challenges it faces.

I wrote this book because I believe everyone has the ability, opportunity, and responsibility to stand out when it matters most.

Throughout my lifetime, I've been fascinated by the people who always seem to get ahead, be in the right place at the right time, have the most luck, and appear to be blessed with special powers and skills reserved for only the chosen few.

On the other hand, I've witnessed the confusion, uncertainty, and stress in aspiring, young students and professionals at every school and company that I've visited or worked for. To make matters worse, schools and companies around the world do a poor job of preparing the younger generation for success and happiness beyond the basics of a selected major, early work experience, extracurricular activities, leadership courses, and other standard career development topics. Millions of high potential young adults get thrown into life without the required tools they need to face the challenges, expectations, and competition they will face. Like many before them, they do their best to figure it out as they go.

Throughout my career and even today as a successful executive, entrepreneur, author, husband, and dad, I face many similar challenges. In some respects, it should be comforting to know that no matter how successful you are, we are all human and life is ever changing and complex. Thus, we all face the same challenges.

Fortunately, challenges can be transformed into opportunities and life is beautiful with its limitless range of possibilities for positive outcomes. Although some situations in life are more impactful than others, no singular moment in life is do or die, nothing is forever, and hope and answers are always available.

THE PLAYBOOK

At its core, this book is a framework for preparing you for success and happiness, while also providing you with a set of guiding principles to help you face the challenges of life head on.

There is already an abundance of information related to personal development available to you. But with that incredibly vast amount of wisdom comes a feeling of being overwhelmed and confused about where to start, what to focus on, and what to do first...until now.

This book was written to inspire, help, and coach you through that infinite maze of knowledge. It will provide you with a new mindset, easy-to-remember action items, and a framework you can use to focus on the most meaningful things. More importantly, it will tell you what you need, what to ignore, and how everything links together.

As you move through each chapter, you'll be building a play-book for your life, step-by-step, to serve three core human needs—clarity, simplicity, and certainty.

With better clarity, you know more, understand more, and feel more confident about the future.

With more simplicity, you think about and focus on the most important things. This reduces confusion and creates a sense of calm.

With higher certainty, you increase the possibilities for success and happiness.

With more success and happiness, you will be able to stand out!

A concise graphic representation of this playbook is included in Appendix A. It is a clear, simple, and powerful way to go from where you are (just starting or restarting) to where you want to go (standing out), by helping you answer nine fundamental questions. You will notice that these questions align perfectly with the playbook, which aligns perfectly with the chapters in this book.

To help you remember the playbook, these steps form the acronym "STANDOUTX."

- **S**elf—Who am I?
- **T**omorrow—Where am I going?
- **A**ttitude—What do I think, believe, and feel?
- **N**ow—What is my purpose, and how do I live it today?
- **D**o—How do I get to where I want to go?
- **O**ptimize—What specific things should I do to make the most of my opportunities?
- **U**plift—How do I lead to help others?
- **T**ouch—How can I make an impact in the world?
- **X**-Factors—How do I stand out?

As you read and work through each chapter of the book, you will gain the necessary knowledge to answer these key questions. You will also become equipped to take the necessary actions on your way to standing out.

Beyond this book and throughout your life, you will receive a lot of advice, guidance, and information from the people you meet and experiences you have. The beauty of the STANDOUTX framework is that it serves as a way to process all those inputs, shows how all the advice fits together, and enables you to see the bigger picture. You will know where to plug-and-play what you learn into your personal and customized playbook to stand out in the game of life.

This book is not written exclusively for students and young professionals. It's also ideal for anyone else who wants a new beginning. Sometimes, like an arrow, you need to be taken back as far as you can go to create the required momentum to launch you forward again.

This book is also for anyone who is in a position to help someone else become a standout. Whether you're a parent, teacher, coach, counselor, consultant, or leader, this book and the associated playbook is structured in a way that provides you with a step-by-step process to guide and coach your up-and-comer. Use the playbook to focus on what's important and add your own life lessons, experiences, advice, and words of wisdom to give it more meaning for you and your mentee.

The strength and power of this playbook is that it also works well for businesses, particularly for those that are starting or need a restart (See Appendix B). By asking similar questions in a similar structure, a company can take the necessary steps to stand out in a competitive market or industry.

- **S**elf—Who and what is the company (mission, vision, core values, and what it offers)?
- **T**omorrow—Where is the company going and why (future benefits and goals)?
- **A**ttitude—What is the company's culture (feeling, standards, and expectations)?
- **N**ow—How does the company collect and analyze data, and how does it apply that knowledge today to fulfill its purpose?
- **D**o—How does the company execute its strategy most efficiently?
- **O**ptimize—How does the company build the critical foundations for success (infrastructure and processes)?
- **U**plift—How does the company hire, train, and develop the employees and its leaders to be their best?
- **T**ouch—How does the company provide world-class customer experiences?
- **X**-Factors—What is the company's competitive advantage and how does it stand out?

Ultimately, this book is for you, and this is your playbook because it's your life to live. Since everyone is different and everyone leads their own lives, you get to fill in the playbook for what works for you. You get to personalize and customize it for who you are and what you need.

The Standout Experience is a carefully crafted collection of the best thoughts, ideas, advice, and recommended actions collected from the experts and people who have paved the way before you. It's also a culmination of the lessons I've personally learned from the many challenging and difficult years I had while being in your shoes.

WHAT IT MEANS TO STAND OUT

Standing out is not a one-time event. It takes years of preparation and hard work that culminates in a particular moment and beyond. Once you get to that moment of truth, the game is already won or lost. That stand-out opportunity is the realization of everything that has come before it.

To prepare you for those key moments, you need to have a vision, strategy, and game plan. Like any great team, you also need to have a playbook to know what to do, how, when, and why. This book is that critical playbook for anyone just starting or restarting.

Since early in elementary school, you've been told repeatedly how crucial it is to work really hard, take a certain path to success, be good to others, and say and do all the right things. While these skills remain critically important to learn, they just scratch the surface of what's required to stand out in today's competitive environment.

To stand out is to emerge from the herd of others struggling to follow the same, worn-out and weather-beaten path to success and happiness, which was first paved by well-meaning, but somewhat narrowly focused people from many generations ago.

Instead of blindly following that pack with no personal awareness of where you want to go, what you want to do, or who you want to be, this book encourages you to forge your own path to success. You may or may not end up at the same destination as others, but that's OK. No matter what happens, you'll enjoy traveling your own journey, custom made to optimize the spirit of your individuality.

Parents, teachers, counselors, and even good friends have great intentions when they try to steer you toward a certain direction. In fact, you might feel a sense of failure if you can't measure up to their idea of success.

You might have a vastly different idea of what success looks like for you. If so, that's fantastic! I urge you to embrace your individuality and leverage all your unique skills to the best of your ability. That is what most accurately reflects the Standout Experience, because it will allow the best version of yourself to rise, shine, and impact.

To stand out is to be different, elevate above the rest, and live the Standout Creed (See Appendix C). To stand out is to increase the probability for success and happiness, whether it's getting that dream job, dating that special someone, or leaving a legacy that outlives your physical existence.

The bottom line is, whatever success looks like to you, the journey starts with one simple notion—your willingness and ability to make the most out of all the wonderfully unique qualities within yourself. You can and will show everyone what makes you special, which is great because we need you to help make the world a better place.

So, how do you make such an impact? How do you become the best possible version of yourself? How do you begin your standout journey?

The answers to those questions are not as easy as most would like them to be. First of all, there is no one prescriptive way to stand out. Each situation and person are different.

With that said, I've discovered some broad themes that all standouts share.

For example, standouts exceed the expectations of others and themselves. They have a positive and significant impact on others and an undeniable ability to move emotions wherever they go. Perhaps most significantly, standouts go beyond themselves and provide lasting value to others.

Standouts shine by creating more opportunities than others, understanding which moments matter most, and being prepared to capitalize on them when given the chance. This book will help you to be just as resourceful, aware, and prepared for your moments.

SETTING EXPECTATIONS

The Standout Experience is about discovery, hope, opportunity, preparation, and meaning. It's about understanding who you are and what you are capable of. It's about creating a vision for yourself and developing a roadmap towards that vision. It's about being different, thinking different, and doing different things. It's also about defining your success, being happy, and living life on your terms. It's about planning, practicing, and perfecting. It's about assuming an indispensable leadership role for others and giving your gifts back to the world. It's about being the chosen one for what the moment requires.

With that said, I'd like to provide a disclaimer about a few things this book isn't.

Throughout these pages, you will not see any ridiculous

claim about one specific thing that you *must* do to achieve success and happiness. The truth is that different strategies, approaches, and ideas work for different people. That's part of the unpredictable beauty and randomness of the world in which we live. Many so-called self-help gurus, life coaches, and experts claim to have discovered the one key aspect of success. I am not one of those people.

I believe that there is no such thing as a universal key to success. There's only your key, which is different from everyone else's. This book aims to help you find that key. When you discover it, you can use it to unlock as many doors for opportunity as possible.

This book is also not going to continue the bombardment of information and advice concerning the basic steps to take to start your career like interviewing, networking, working hard, and other basic skills. These are considered *table stakes* that everyone must do. They're important, but they only get you a seat at the table. To stand out, you need to be able to play a winning hand when it matters most, no matter what cards you're dealt.

This book is also not meant to be a complete work of everything you will ever need to know. If it was, this book would read more like a long and grueling to-do list of tactics and advice. Instead, it's a synthesized framework for you to take with you on the long and wonderful journey that you have ahead of you.

Finally, this book isn't based on scientific research, and it doesn't present the results of a major university study. It does, however, present an abundance of new ideas, thought processes, and actionable steps to help you on your journey to standing out.

Some of those ideas and action steps may seem familiar, like you've read or heard them before. If so, that's great, because the more you're exposed to the same thing, the more your brain takes notice and prioritizes that information to a higher level of importance.

Keep in mind that common sense and common advice aren't always common practice and it doesn't always lead to uncommon results. Raising the importance of something that seems like common sense forces you to think differently and makes you take actions you might not normally take. By taking these actions and gaining years of wisdom in the few short hours or days it will take to read this book, you'll accelerate your potential and gain a competitive advantage over everyone else.

IT'S GAME TIME!

I can't guarantee that reading this book will mysteriously create a satisfying and fulfilling life or make you stand out. It's not a magic wand. You still have to put in the time to think about what you read and put in a lot of hard work, but the results will be well worth the investment.

In the next few chapters, you'll learn a little more about my story and where I've come from. You'll also learn how you and I may have more in common than you realize.

In a later chapter, you'll read about a foundational concept of this book, which is to treat life as a competitive, interesting, and addictively fun game. Rather than stressing out about life, I advise you to become energized by the challenge and enjoy it!

When you look at life as a game, you understand that there are always more chances to move forward and succeed, even if you get knocked backward or need to start over once in a while. The truly amazing thing about life is that opportunities to succeed in various ways continue into your thirties, forties, fifties, and beyond. But you're not going to get there by doing nothing. You need to take action, and now is the best possible time to do so.

Are you ready to play? We have a lot of material to cover, but soon you'll have an advantage that I wish I had when I was younger. If only there was a guide that could have helped me to prevent some of my mistakes. Entire generations before you feel the same way, wishing they had something to help them stand out when it matters most, and guide them through the more challenging moments of their lives as well. Fortunately, that won't be you.

Game on!

PART 1

CLARITY

"There is nothing quite as intense as the moment of clarity when you suddenly see what's really possible for you."

~CHRISTINE LANE

WRITE YOUR
STORY

①

"You write your life story by the choices you make."

~HELEN MIRREN

Let's start with the simple fact that this is your life and you're the only one who lives it. Yes, your life has an impact on others, and you live within a broader world, but it's still your life to live. How you live that life is the culmination of all the decisions you make every day. This is an important idea because it's contrary to what you or others might think. Life doesn't happen to you; it happens because of you, and it happens for you.

No one controls your life but you. You decide what you do and don't do every day. If the uncontrollable and unthinkable happens, you choose how to react.

When writing this life story, nobody else holds the pen. You determine how the story progresses and how it ends.

Not only do you get to write your story, but you also get to edit it. If something doesn't go your way, you can try it again, change it, or delete it.

If something is missing, you can create whatever you need.

Another way to think about this is the quote from Ziad Abdelnour: "Life is like a camera. Focus on what's important and capture the good times. If things don't work out, take another shot."

YOUR ROLE

Everyone is unique in this world, and no one travels the

same path. Thus, your story is uniquely about you. You get to play the role you choose and walk the path nobody else walks.

Donald Miller, the American author and CEO of StoryBrand, talks about how we play four roles in our life, just like there are four characters in every story. You can either be the victim, the villain, the guide, or the hero.

Others will play roles in your story. Some are like ships passing in the night; others are key characters who shape and influence your life. Still others are dear to you and might walk the journey with you. You decide which characters play the roles in your story.

Unfortunately, some people play a victim role and live a story that's given to them, as if it's being read to them while they go to sleep at night, and all they have to do is follow the words— verbatim—when they wake up in the morning.

Others, however, stand out and choose to write their own story. They decide which paths to take or create their own path. These individuals decide which people they impact (and how) and the difference they make in the world. Their story is not yet written, because they are the authors with society playing the role of supporting cast, not the all-powerful determining source of how the story begins, unfolds, and ends. We admire their courage and bravery, and wish we were like them.

Which life story would you rather live? Do you want the one that's handed to you, where you play a victim role and don't choose the direction of your life? Do you want to leave your story to chance, or worse, in the hands of someone else? Or, would you prefer to play the hero role and write the pages from beginning to end?

The latter is the story chosen by the person who wants to stand out. As the great philosopher, Marshall McLuhan said, "There are no passengers on Spaceship Earth. We're all crew."

Your journey and your life story are about you. In order to play that character, you have to be that character. You can't try to be someone else. It's hard enough to be yourself, let alone trying to be someone you're not.

Whether you believe it yet or not, you were born to do incredible things. To accomplish those incredible things, you have to be you, break away from the mold, take control of the things you have power over, and stop worrying about things that you don't. You have the potential to turn the victim into a hero, a hero into a guide, and a guide into a legend.

Before you do great things, you must have the awareness of who you are (your character), the clarity to know where you 're going (the storyline), and the hunger to author that version of your story (the control to overcome the hero's struggle). Who you think you are and the character you play will determine how you show up in the world.

MY STORY

At one time, I wasn't doing any of those things or living my own story. In fact, I'm not sure if I was living any story at all. I was wandering aimlessly with no real direction or meaning to my life. I was lost, confused, and existing but not really living.

My struggle concerned not only the challenges with life itself, which we all face, but I added unnecessary difficulties to my situation as well. At the time, I didn't realize that I had ultimate control over everything I did do or didn't do, as well as how I reacted to all of life's circumstances.

If any of that sounds like you, don't worry. There's no need to feel overly stressed, pressured, or anxious about it. Those are all perfectly natural emotions, but that's not the way anybody wants to feel forever, and nobody has to, because your story is just beginning.

Through wisdom and experience, I've learned that my entire life has been and always will be completely in my control. Clearly, we all face similar certainties of life. I'm not talking about death, taxes, and data breaches. I'm talking about all the discomfort and struggles that people don't post on social media.

Life is hard, unpredictable, and fragile. It's full of challenging moments, difficult choices, and missed opportunities. After all, there are eight billion people in the world and an infinite universe of possibilities exists. That alone means that life can't be simple or without problems.

On the surface, it might seem that others have it figured out, or seem to easily evade any serious challenges or issues. You only see the onstage persona that others want you to see, and you only see what's broadcast in the news or posted on social media. You see the polished results, but never a glimpse of the hardships faced previous to their success or the countless rehearsals they endured behind the scenes. Thus, as Teddy Roosevelt once said, "Comparison is the thief of joy." To be relevant to you, you need to know their backstory behind their success story.

For example, you might see my titles and experiences as an executive for Walt Disney or Madison Square Garden and think I was on the corporate fast track from day one. You could dig a little deeper to discover that I graduated with honors from two high-profile schools, finished multiple marathons, wrote this book, and founded a personal development, leadership, and impact company. Those successes may enhance your first impression of me as one of those individuals who has always had life figured out and steered clear of any difficulties.

What the first impression of almost everyone (including myself) doesn't reveal, however, is the hard work and specific investments that were made over a long period of time. Others never see the blood, sweat, and tears that are invested in private to enable the results that are seen in public. They don't see the tough choices, sacrifices, hardships, and challenges that come with living the human experience in a complex world.

Career and life are not singular, long, upward sloping lines to success. There are moments of growth, more money, better titles, and increased responsibility. But there are also moments when you must make tough decisions, take a step backwards, push harder to continue the upward momentum, or fight through periods of stagnation.

YOUR PLAN
Easy and Straightforward

REALITY
Successes and Challenges

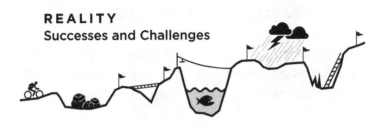

The path to success is filled with many ups and downs that come with the journey itself, particularly when you look at your life at the micro level. Those daily fluctuations are actually a great thing, however, because they mean you're alive. Otherwise, you would be flatlining and that's no way to truly live.

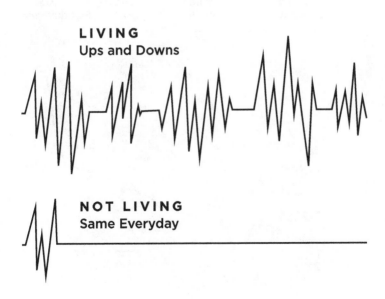

LIVING
Ups and Downs

NOT LIVING
Same Everyday

A quick glance at my resume certainly doesn't convey any of the challenges and issues I faced (and continue to face) that got me to this point. Just like everyone else, my reality was not an easy and straightforward journey to the top.

As I share the various stages of my own life with the many challenges I've faced in each of them, my hope is you'll understand that you're not alone. You'll also see that I didn't have that magical life-altering event that other high-profile thought leaders and successful people have had.

It took me years of trial and error, successes and failures, wrong turns, and adjustments to learn what it takes to succeed and be happy. More importantly, I learned firsthand of the importance of standing out when it matters most. Thankfully, you only need to read this book and make the choice now to be a standout in your own life.

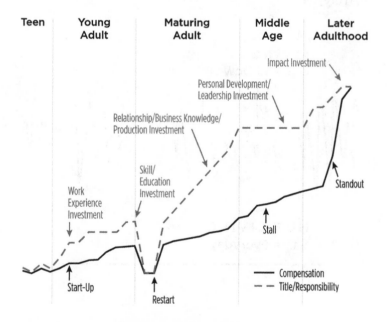

THE CHALLENGES OF ADOLESCENCE

Things beyond your control will undoubtedly happen to you throughout your lifetime—the death of a loved one, parents who get divorced, layoffs, major weather events, and the effects of another person's choices. We're all impacted by things that happen around us.

My parents got divorced when I was a teenager, and I found myself battling periods of homelessness during and after high school. I lived in nearby homes that were under construction, stayed inside neighborhood carports, slept outside the local train depot, spent a few nights at friends' houses, and showered in the break room of the restaurant where I sometimes worked. Other nights, I walked the streets or the railroad tracks aimlessly just to keep warm.

I attended school on occasion (probably missed more than half of my senior year in high school) and still don't know how I graduated on time. When I found someone to live with, the people I trusted took everything from me, not once, not twice, but three times. I lost all my personal possessions and all the money I made while working night shifts, holidays, and weekends for years before and during high school.

Over time and without any idea of who I was or what I wanted, I tried various careers in hospitality, music, law, airlines, food service, office services, coaching, and computers. I felt the stress of living paycheck to paycheck and often went days without food or shelter. No direction or purpose to my life existed. I was lazy, immature, and lacked a work ethic that kept me employed for more than a few months at a time. Truthfully, I was fired by more jobs than I care to admit.

At various points, my strong ambition got the best of me and I attempted community college, but like my attempts at working, I flunked out (more than once) with a 0.00 GPA.

I started to party too much with my friends and while that provided temporary relief, it could have been a very dark and lonely road that I thankfully didn't travel. I also experienced the joys of marriage and the pains of divorce and other failed relationships.

Before I go any further, I want to make it extremely clear that it would be easy to blame my parents, bosses, teachers, friends, and exes for those situations and the painful feelings that came with them, but that would be wrong.

In hindsight, it's clear that I was in control of my actions and I influenced the decisions they made. The outcomes that impacted me were mine alone. Still, the challenges at the time were real, the situations were difficult, and the emotions were raw and hurtful.

With those challenges came my first insight and awareness into the concept of standing out. I often wondered why certain moments, certain people, and certain events stayed with me (good or bad), and why others were irrelevant and not worth remembering. This started my journey of exploration and curiosity on the road to learning why certain people and events stand out.

THE UNCERTAINTIES OF EARLY ADULTHOOD

Regardless of the paths you choose, you will face many truths in life. Two of them are uncertainty and risk.

No job can ensure sustainable success or lifelong employment, people will come and go, and opportunities may or may not be present at any given time. Nobody can ever know what the future holds. Therefore, uncertainty is a given. In order to move forward with uncertainty, you must accept some level of risk-taking. The question is how much risk should you be willing to take and when?

In my mid-twenties, when everyone I knew had finished school, started their careers, and some had even gotten married, I settled into a steady job with a good salary working for a law firm in Washington, D.C. Thinking I wanted to be a lawyer at the time, this seemed like a logical step in the right direction.

Initially, I was hired as a mail clerk but with a strong work ethic and a desire to learn, grow, and take on new challenges, I moved into a role as a project manager, where I assisted with research, court filings, and other legal matters while also helping manage office services. I established myself as a high-performer and I was content but far from happy. Nonetheless, I had enough money to afford a decent apartment, a nice car, and I bought other nice-to-have things. I had a girlfriend, and life really wasn't that bad. It was steady and comfortable but still lacked something.

After spending far too long in that mode of nothingness, I ultimately decided that I wanted more.

I had progressed enough in my role that I felt stuck between where I had been and where I wanted to go. The people around me were either living their basic, day-to-day lives in various support roles or they were the highly ambitious and successful attorneys that we worked with. Further, there were certain attorneys and partners who had something special and they always seemed to be in the right place at the right time, working on the best cases with the best clients.

For the second time, I became acutely aware and highly focused on the concept of standing out. I often wondered how and why certain people stood out while others didn't. What did they do? What did they have? What was their secret sauce?

At some point, I became fascinated by people who stood out to me, and a feeling that I wanted to be just like them started to build inside me.

With the inspiring people around me and a clearer idea or vision of what was possible for my own future, I decided to face my own uncertainty and insecurities and go "all-in" on getting a college degree.

I set specific goals to graduate by a certain date, set the bar for a 4.0 GPA, and dreamed of going to the best public university in the country at the University of Virginia. I was going to make up for lost time and prove that I could be as successful as anyone else.

TAKING RISKS IN EARLY ADULTHOOD

So many students and young professionals focus on going to that one top school, getting that one perfect internship, and landing that ideal first job. The reality is that early adulthood is the time to experiment, try new things, and gain new experiences. It's a time to figure out what you like and don't like, what you're good at, and what you're not good at. More importantly, it's a time to take risks while you have so many years to recover and restart if you need to.

Similarly, I decided to take a risk and walk away from all of the comforts that I had, all of the people I knew, and all the money I was making for the faith that something bigger and better was coming. It wasn't an easy choice. So many people told me that I was crazy, and I would never get into UVA with my prior GPA history despite my recent successes. This was the third time that the concept of standing out became very real for me.

To get into a school like UVA with my cumulative GPA and high school transcript (and test scores), I had to show that I was different, sell my unique story, and share the vision of my future self.

I prepared a fifty-page, college entrance legal brief (with all of the necessary exhibits, references, and arguments) requesting admission to UVA, and drove it to Charlottesville in a driving rainstorm. The brief was full of data, graphs, trendlines, comparative statistics, carefully worded arguments, and previous student stories that compared to mine.

The look on the face of the admissions director when I dropped it off, introduced myself, told my thirty-second story, and said, "I can't wait to be here again when I start school next January," was priceless. The standout admissions packet worked.

Once I got to Charlottesville, I maintained a laser focus on my goals and worked towards a vision of my future self. I graduated with distinction (honors), and had multiple offers from investment banks, consulting firms, and Fortune 500 companies.

While my classmates and friends took these "sexy" roles in New York, Chicago, and other high-profile locations, I decided to take a risk and move to Orlando to start my career with Disney.

I didn't make as much money as others, and my role wasn't as prestigious, but the job did fit the lifestyle I wanted. The company's values matched my own personal core values, and I had a lot of room for future growth and development.

Over the next nine years, I performed my job to the best of my ability. I took on new projects and challenges with optimism and excitement, and I surrounded myself with the right people. I was also motivated by a core value to be different and driven by a deep desire to stand out from the rest.

I was further motivated by the fact that I could help others around me to be successful. My mindset and value system allowed me to progress quickly through the organization, which led to an executive role in about nine years. Clearly, the risks I took were paying off.

SELF-DISCOVERY IN MIDDLE ADULTHOOD

Wisdom that's been passed down from previous generations tells us that past experience can be an indicator of future success. With that in mind, my trajectory at Disney left me feeling that I was nowhere near my potential and the upside was unlimited.

I did all the things my leaders, mentors, and peers advised me to do. They told me to keep working really hard, leverage my strengths, recognize opportunities, take on big projects, do great work, be loyal to the company, learn the business, and be a team player. They advised me that by doing all those things in a consistently excellent manner, my time would come.

That was great advice by many well-intentioned people, but isn't that what everyone is supposed to do? Isn't that what everyone who gets hired tries to do? Within that notion exists a hidden problem.

Everyone else around me at Disney was also talented and following similar advice. It's no wonder that at some point, the funnel gets smaller and what got me to that point wasn't going to get me to where I wanted to go. By doing the same things I had been doing and with such immense talent around me, I stayed at the same level for eight more years.

This is when I had my next standout realization. I had plateaued, and it was clear that I was in familiar company with other exceptional, strong, high-performing, and high-potential executives. What was the great separator among us, and why did a few of us move on to the next level while I and others hadn't?

Putting my hopes on someone else's decision about me wasn't working, and I needed to take control by doing something different. The advice I was getting was the antithesis of what I needed to do to be able to sit at the table.

The fuel I needed to propel myself further came from a letter my leader placed on my desk two days before Christmas. That simple act of constructive feedback started me on a "next level" journey in my career.

That letter stated that I was a highly valuable, high-performing, and well-liked leader in the organization, but I needed to work on a few things before I moved into higher-level roles.

The note was well-intentioned, but the way it was delivered and written with some difficult-to-hear feedback seemed more like a performance letter. It was an untimely punch to the gut that I took the wrong way as a bruise to my work ego. I became angry, confused, and unsure of my future.

In hindsight, the letter was exactly what I needed, and it put me on a path to self-discovery, personal development, leadership growth, and a focus on having a positive impact on other people instead of working for my own self gain. The letter suggested a few books and articles, recommended a leadership development course, instructed me to get an executive coach, and assigned a mentor to me.

I decided to use that letter as a wakeup call to stop resting on my past successes and become that hungry, ambitious kid again.

From there, I worked tirelessly to take every worthwhile self-development and leadership course that I could find. I became a ferocious reader and listened to two to three podcasts every day in a continuous effort to enhance my skills. As a leader, I interviewed hundreds of other high performers inside and outside the company. I spent hours with my executive coach, got advice from multiple mentors, and studied the "best of the best" in the company. To this day, I'm always learning, growing, and striving to be better.

This heavy investment in myself became the inputs that changed my outputs. My performance reviews were even better than before.

New possibilities presented themselves in my current company, and I received interest about opportunities from other organizations and industries as well. I met new people, and the new person that I became even helped introduce me to my wonderful, amazing, and beautiful wife. Soon after, I became a guest lecturer and keynote speaker at different universities on personal development and leadership.

Eventually, my leadership took notice of the change and I was chosen to take a higher-level executive role to help launch Disney+ in New York City. I truly appreciated the short time I spent there, and I learned a lot about what's necessary to take a business from starting up to standing out.

COMMITMENT AND DEDICATION OF MATURE ADULTHOOD

So often in your own life, you will seize a moment that will lead to another unforeseen opportunity if you just take that first step. Not long after I moved to NYC and was working at Disney+, another opportunity presented itself to leave Disney. After more than eighteen years with a company that I loved and an organization that held enormous growth potential for me, I had to consider making another difficult (and risky) decision.

After a lot of thought (and a few sleepless nights), I decided to walk away from the career path, people, and pension that Disney offered to take a new opportunity with Madison Square Garden (MSG). If I was ever going to see what it's like to work for a new company, with new people, and in a new environment, this was it. This wasn't the first time that I made a bold move for my future success and happiness, nor will it be the last. The decision paid off, literally and figuratively.

I learned that you get out of life what you put into it. If you spend the time on yourself, have a vision of your future, and commit yourself to disciplined execution, you will get what you want.

When others told me repeatedly that the greatest investment you will ever make is in yourself, I listened but never really followed up on it. Now, I can tell you—without question or hesitation—that the time, effort, and energy you put into yourself will return exponential dividends later. It will make you a better person and a better leader. That investment will also help you to make a greater difference in the lives of the people and businesses around you. As Ralph Waldo Emerson said, "The only person that you are destined to become is the person that you decide to be."

By looking at my current career and position in life, it might look like I've made it and there is no further work for me to do. However, in order to truly stand out, I must keep moving forward and reach for the things that feel unreachable at times.

There is always another level if your vision is clear, you

work relentlessly on improving yourself, and you implement a game plan that drives you from Point A to Point B and beyond.

I wish I would have had a better understanding for the promise that the future held when I was younger. If nothing else, it would have made the journey much easier and definitely less stressful. Having GPS guidance with turn-by-turn navigation to a distinct destination is always much better than getting into a moving vehicle with no hands on the wheel, hoping it arrives at a satisfactory location.

One last point on moving forward, there is not one and only one destination or purpose for anybody. With all of the infinite possibilities in this world, how sad would it be to know that you were predestined to have just one outcome? Thankfully, that's not the case.

You're in complete control of your life. New challenges and opportunities to be better exist all around you. To get there, however, you need to always be moving forward, have faith, and do what's right and best for you and your future self. As Albert Einstein said, "Life is like a bicycle, to keep your balance you must keep moving."

LEAVING A LEGACY IN LATE ADULTHOOD

No matter what you accomplish, it's human nature to look back and wonder "what if?" For instance, what if you had taken that one job your friend told you about? What if you had dated that person you met in college? What if you hadn't moved so far away from home? What if you studied more? What if you exercised regularly and ate better? However, dwelling on the past won't help you in the future. After all, how can you move on to the next chapter if you keep reading the last one?

Instead of constantly wondering "what if" about the past and getting stuck in the fear of missing out, say, "what if" as you focus on the future, set a course for a specific destination, and create unlimited opportunities down the road. Saying those two words and shifting your mindset from what choices were behind you to what's possible in front of you should inspire a feeling of hopeful excitement as you continue moving forward.

My "what if" is focused on the legacy that I will someday leave behind. It's about the difference I can make in the lives of people around me. I choose to welcome the future potential I can create with every action moving forward.

You never know what's coming next, but you always have the power to do something about it. It's up to you to imagine the possibilities, plan appropriately, and prepare for that standout moment when you hit the stage in front of the right people at the right time.

It's impossible to stand out if you dwell on the past or perform the same actions as everyone else. You were born with a different genetic makeup than any of the other eight billion people in the world. Each day, not only do you live a life that no one else has lived before, but you are also capable of accomplishing amazingly unique things.

When crafting the story of your life, use your past as fuel for your present, and consider your present as the starting point for your future. From there, envision your future as a beacon for where you want to go and who you want to become.

Also, always remember that nothing in your story is written in stone. You can edit individual words, whole paragraphs, and entire chapters as often as necessary.

KNOWING WHAT'S IMPORTANT

Before we close this chapter, let's make sure we address an important topic...success.

Early in my career, I thought success was money, titles, and what others thought of me. I worked hard to recover from my past and prove to others that I was successful. When I tasted success, I always wanted more, but I was losing perspective.

With society's version of success comes emptiness and a feeling of "what's next?" After a while, you realize that there will never be enough.

When you achieve that next goal, it becomes your new normal. Soon, you want something more or different. Psychology calls this hedonic adaptation. This is the term to describe what happens when you achieve something and the feeling of accomplishment fades as you subconsciously reset to the new standard. It's a frustrating cycle that repeats itself.

With the wrong focus on success, you also lose perspective on what's really important. This realization hit me hard after I started working at MSG and thought I had made it. That once homeless kid in Virginia had become a senior executive in NYC. Then one spring break, it all changed.

I was taking my daughter to the airport to put her on a plane back to Florida, where she would be with her mom. After a tearful goodbye, I watched her walk onto the plane and I just stood there. Looking to my right, out the window, I watched the snow start to fall.

The plane backed away, got de-iced, and then taxied to the runway. Within a few hundred feet of taking off, the plane disappeared into the clouds. I sat down on a chair near the gate and I lost it. As tears poured down my face, I started to ask myself, "What am I doing?" Even when I seemingly had it all, I felt lost and confused again like that young kid a long time ago.

It was in that moment I realized that success and happiness are what you determine them to be, not what society says or what others think they are. That's when I made the choice to make success in my own life more holistic, including spending more time with the people who matter most in my life. I also decided that my success would be determined by the success of others around me, not by money, titles, or career achievements.

STAIRS

At the end of each chapter, you will find a series of Standout Thoughts, Actions, Ideas, Reflections, and Steps (STAIRS) for you to think about, write in your journal, discuss with someone else, and do in your own life.

These are three to five high-level ideas that support your singular goal with each chapter. They are considered STAIRS because you take them one at a time on your climb to standing out. Each one is an opportunity to build on toward the next one.

By no means are these an exhaustive and complete list of things to think about and do, but they are some of the most important ideas. Hopefully, these STAIRS will give you the key steps that you can take to implement the chapter ideas, and they might generate other ideas that work better for you.

The key is to understand this particular part of the playbook, think about what it means for you, and do something to put the broader idea into action on your way to standing out.

Visit www.standoutmovement.com for more STAIRS and detailed worksheets to download. You can also share what you learned, what you did, and what results you got so that it can benefit others. The key is to not just read these chapters; that's what ordinary people do but not you.

You are the Standout Experience because you are taking these ideas, making them your own, helping others, and doing the work that others won't so that you can have what others don't, and do what others can't when it matters most.

STAIRS TO HELP YOU WRITE YOUR STORY

Today:

- Identify the things in your life that you can control and rate yourself on how well you control them. What can you do differently to take more control?
- Of the things you think you can't control, how would your

best self respond, what can you avoid, and what can you possibly take ownership of?

- Find other people's inspiring stories and learn what they did to own their life, take risks, and capitalize on opportunities.
- Write a short story about your ideal life. What character did you play and what was your heroic journey?

Every day:

- At night, reflect on your day and take note of what you controlled and what controlled you. How did you respond? Did you own the day?
- Design your tomorrow. How can you be more intentional? Where can you take ownership of your calendar? And how will you advance your goals? Where can you create more productive time and how will you use it?
- Pick something to do that's hard, uncomfortable, and risky but advances you to the next chapter of your story (closer to your goals).
- Share your story with others and celebrate your successes while also learning from your failures and mistakes. You get better either way and you never know who you will inspire.

Main goal: Seize control of your life, own your future, and write your own story.

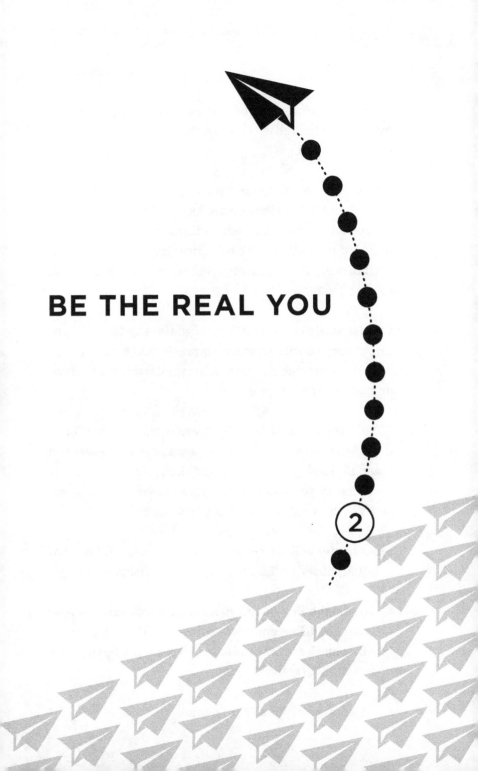

BE THE REAL YOU

"You are very powerful, provided you know how powerful you are."

~YOGI BAHAMAN

All great stories are written with a vivid description of the main character, and in this great story of your life, the main character is you.

As you begin creating your story, you first need to know who you are, not just on the surface level or through some pre-conceived notion of who others think you are or want you to be but the real you. It's of critical importance to know what makes you tick, how you feel, what you like, and what you don't like.

You also need to know that the real you is okay. Like the hero in any story, you have flaws, weaknesses, and shortcomings. You also have some unique qualities and strengths to shine on the world around you.

Finally, you should know about you in the future. Who is that ideal person you want to be to achieve your goals and dreams? We all grow, develop, and change in some respects over time. Do you stand out by expressing who you really are now and working towards who you want to be later?

This chapter will impact you with three powerful tools to help you shine that light as brightly as you can:

1. **Hindsight.** Reacquaint yourself with your past and your inner child. Remember the things you did that led to victories and learn from the mistakes you made, so you don't repeat them going forward.

2. **Insight.** Understand your present. What are your thoughts, key skills, and superpowers? What do you like and don't like? What are you good at and not good at? How do you feel about your place in the world? How do you interact with others? These are important questions to answer that will provide you with a healthy foundation of self-awareness.

3. **Foresight.** Get to know who you want to be in the near and distant future. To achieve your future dreams and goals, you first need to become the person who is capable of achieving everything you want in life.

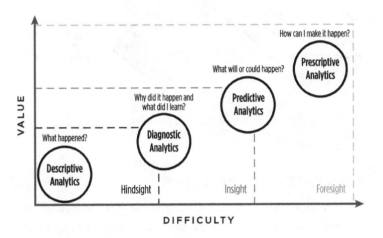

There is tremendous value in these three tools. They help you to understand who you truly are and live as the real you every day. These tools help you live from the inside out, not outside in. They also help you to use your past as fuel, your present as the vehicle in which you're traveling, and the future as a roadmap to get to where you want to go.

Remember that you are a unique diamond in the rough, waiting to shine your brilliance for others to see. A diamond is the perfect mental image for you to think about every day, because it points in four directions:

- Backward to remind you where you've been.
- Downward to ground you in the present moment.
- Forward to tell you to keep moving, no matter what happens.
- Upward to inspire you to rise to your greatest potential.

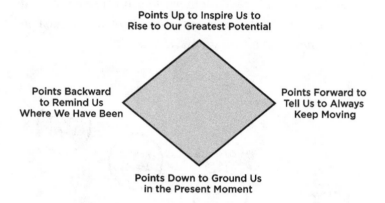

YOUR PAST (NATURAL) SELF

You probably don't realize it, but you have stood out before. Early in your past, you did all the things unknowingly that the self-help books and personal development mentors of today tell you to do.

From birth to around ten years old, you were yourself because you didn't yet know of any other way to be.

As a kid, you believed you could do anything and had no fear. If you got hurt, you wore that scar—whether physical or emotional—like a badge of honor. Your natural state was happiness, and you had an insatiable appetite for exploration and discovery.

Almost every day you laughed and cried often, as you became acquainted with the full spectrum of human emotions.

You lived by your own rules, had boundless energy, and never stopped moving.

You enjoyed every moment and were never afraid to try new things. If you failed (like when learning to walk), you laughed it off and tried again.

You shared a contagious love and connection with your parents, relatives, schoolmates, and the world around you.

You enjoyed your successes and celebrated them with family and friends.

You also learned from the things you did as your parents taught you right from wrong.

If you did it before, you can do it again.

Living as a standout means reflecting on your past, evaluating what worked and what didn't, and applying what you've learned to be better. The best business leaders do it for their companies and the best athletes do it to win games. Standouts in life do it to be their best for themselves and the world around them.

We all have bad days, but standouts always find the lesson

in their past, let it go, and apply it to their future. They also replicate their great days more consistently than others.

Here are some ideas to use your past as fuel for your future.

- Think about one of your best days and write (in as many details as possible) why it was so amazing. How can you replicate those results?
- Think about the moments when you have been at your best. Why were you at your best and how can you replicate that?
- If you had to write your own top ten lessons learned, how can you apply them to today?
- When key moments have gone wrong in your past, why did you not get the result for which you were hoping? What did you learn from the experience, and what can you do differently next time?
- What failures can you use as fuel to propel you forward?
- What other ways can you leverage your past, recreate those greatest moments, apply the lessons you learned, and avoid the mistakes you made?

Prominent New Age thought leader Deepak Chopra proposed incredibly valuable insight when he said, "Every time you are tempted to react in the same old way, ask if you want to be a prisoner of the past or a pioneer of the future."

Standouts are prisoners of nothing—always using the past as fuel, aware of opportunities in the present, and acting as pioneers of the future. Keep in mind that your past is not the only past that can help your future. As Otto von Bismarck said, "Any fool can learn from his mistakes. The wise man learns from the mistakes of others."

YOUR PRESENT SELF

Once you've reacquainted yourself with your natural state of being and how well that aligns with your ability to stand out, you can learn more about who you are today.

At this point of your life, you're likely at a crossroads. Those carefree days of youth are mostly behind you, but you can attempt to tap into that energy and enthusiasm for life again as you move forward.

Standouts have a keen sense for what is happening *in the moment* and what actions they should be taking to maximize their opportunities. They don't let the common distractions of a modern multitasking society like cell phones and social media deter them from their focus on the task at hand.

You too can acknowledge and celebrate all of the amazing things about who you are today. Maybe you're an exceptional student, a hard-working athlete, a tremendously talented musician, or even a kindhearted and approachable soul. Perhaps you're a natural born leader, a great philosopher, or really good at helping others.

If any of those constitute a part of who you are today, that's outstanding! If not, there are a million other ways you could be great. You just need to recognize what they are, so you can leverage them to achieve increasingly higher levels of whatever success looks like for you.

The first victory lap you can take regarding your desire to stand out is that you're reading this book. That means you already understand the importance of the present moment and want to learn everything you can about how to be better in the future. That doesn't mean that you're not already fantastic. It means you can always be better, just like the rest of us (including me). Learning how to stand out is one excellent way to do that.

SELF-ASSESSMENT

In order to effectively get to know the real you in the present, take as many self-assessments as you can. This isn't a one-time event, and the best of the best tend to do these assessments more frequently than the rest.

Some examples of self-assessments include the Myers-Briggs Type Indicator, Strengthfinders, The Enneagram, 360 Degree Surveys, Winslow Personality Profile, Keirsey Temperament Sorter, Big Five Personality Assessment, Holland Code, FIRO-B, DISC Assessment, and a personal SWOT analysis. The more tests and assessments you take and the more quality input and feedback you get from others, the more you will get to know the real you (and how others see you).

A self-assessment that I've done for years is a personalized and customized version of the Wheel of Life used by Tony Robbins and so many other self-help experts. Instead of a simple eight- or ten-point assessment, I created a twenty-five-point assessment that I take once per quarter (four times per year). This allows me to assign a letter grade and GPA based on how I'm doing with each of the twenty-five points, and a 4.0 across the board means that I'm at 100 percent.

Similar assessments use a one through ten scale, but I don't know the difference between a six and seven or a two and three. Since I enjoy the challenge and feedback of "grading" myself, I like to use a standard educational system for the assessment.

This exercise is designed to let you know where you are in your standout journey. Don't worry if you score below your expectations, because this section is only meant to help you determine the areas in which you should concentrate to get closer to the standout person you envision in your future.

There are five parts to this self-assessment.

1. **Interior self.** This part is all about honestly getting to know who you are on the inside. One of my mentors, Robin Sharma, calls it the four interior empires.

2. **Exterior self.** This is about the people, places, and things around you. You are a product of your environment and the average of the five people you spend the most time with. Therefore, this is a critical component.

3. **Your work.** The third section centers around the activities you participate in to make a living and how you help others do the same.

4. **Your inputs.** The fourth section is about your inputs that drive your actions. Take care of your inputs and you will increase the richness of your outputs.

5. **Your outputs.** The last section is about your outputs and the results you get. This section is also how others see, think, and feel about you.

Give yourself a traditional letter grade (A-F) for each of the twenty-five questions. Each result corresponds to the following numerical values:

- A = four points (a strength)
- B = three points (above average)
- C = two points (average)
- D = one point (below average)
- F = zero points (a weakness)

Feel free to give yourself half points wherever you see fit for pluses and minuses. For example, if you think your physical is a solid B+, give yourself three-and-a-half points.

After answering all twenty-five questions, add up the number of points to come up with your total score, which will be between zero and one hundred. In effect, you're scoring a personal GPA (Greatness Personal Assessment).

This assessment is in a particular order, and the categories are purposeful for five primary reasons:

1. You will learn that your power and greatness come from the inside, and the how is shaped by your environment.

2. You will become energized with the confidence of knowing what your strengths are and how they're reflected by others.

3. You will become educated about the key areas that matter to you and those you can work on for future betterment.

4. You will see where your weak points are. If you picture

the twenty-five points as a circle reflective of a tire, you will see where there are "flats" that need to be fixed.

5. Most importantly, you will see that life is holistic. You can't achieve success and happiness if you have areas in your life that are broken. What good is it to have money if you aren't healthy? What good is it to be in love if your lifestyle isn't conducive to having a great relationship?

Realize that no score should be interpreted as poor or failing. If you receive a total grade of fifty-five, which would be interpreted as failing in the traditional sense, this will provide you with a good opportunity to transform your mindset into a more positive frame by understanding the areas you need to improve and committing yourself to taking action.

A few other key points to keep in mind.

First, be sure to answer these questions honestly. Only through accurate self-reflection will you develop a clear understanding for who you are today, which will provide excellent direction on who you want to become tomorrow.

Second, have someone else do the assessment of you. You will see where there are consistencies and gaps in perception.

Third, do the assessment often to measure your progress. You can actually use this tool to develop your goals. Also, as with everything else in this book, have fun with it!

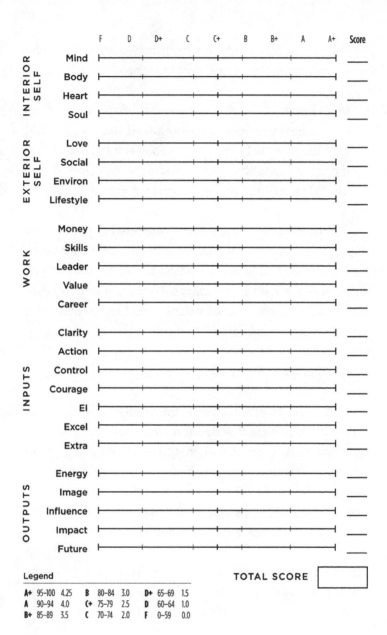

		F	D	D+	C	C+	B	B+	A	A+	Score
INTERIOR SELF	Mind										__
	Body										__
	Heart										__
	Soul										__
EXTERIOR SELF	Love										__
	Social										__
	Environ										__
	Lifestyle										__
WORK	Money										__
	Skills										__
	Leader										__
	Value										__
	Career										__
INPUTS	Clarity										__
	Action										__
	Control										__
	Courage										__
	EI										__
	Excel										__
	Extra										__
OUTPUTS	Energy										__
	Image										__
	Influence										__
	Impact										__
	Future										__

Legend

A+	95–100	4.25	B	80–84	3.0	D+	65–69	1.5
A	90–94	4.0	C+	75–79	2.5	D	60–64	1.0
B+	85–89	3.5	C	70–74	2.0	F	0–59	0.0

TOTAL SCORE

Interior Self

1. **Body.** How do you look and feel from a physical perspective? Is your overall health and conditioning achieving desirable results? Do you have the physical energy, sleep, and nutrition necessary to work effectively throughout your day?

2. **Mind.** How would you rate your overall intelligence, knowledge, and thought process? Are you sharp, focused, and positive?

3. **Heart.** How healthy are your emotions? How do you feel inside? Are you calm, poised, happy, and optimistic?

4. **Soul.** Do you have a sense of something that is bigger than you? It could be a God, the universe, Mother Nature, or life itself, but life is bigger than just you. Are you at peace with that higher purpose?

Exterior Self

5. **Love.** How are your most intimate relationships with your spouse, significant other, partner, and/or kids (if you have them). Do you show them true love, and do you feel deeply loved by them?

6. **Social.** Are you satisfied or fulfilled with your current social circles, such as family, close friends, coworkers, membership organizations, and others in your community?

7. **Environment.** How safe, comfortable, and happy are you with the physical environments in which you spend

the most time (home, work, school, vehicles, social functions, etc.)? This would even include if you read or watch the news. Are you taking in positive messages and information that helps you to grow, or are you surrounded by negativity and people who pull you down? Who is included in your team of coaches, advisors, and mentors?

8. **Lifestyle.** What sort of enjoyment factor is your current lifestyle affording you? Think about what sort of activities in which you regularly participate, such as live music, athletic participation/spectatorship, art museums, reading. This would also include the time spent commuting to and from work. How do you feel about the time you spend on activities outside of work, daily responsibilities, etc.?

Your Work

9. **Money.** Is your current financial situation providing you with stress, or does it allow you to spend money on yourself and others as a means of satisfaction and contribution? Do you follow a budget? Do you save and spend wisely? Do you have a financial plan for the future? Do you have monetary goals? What about your potential earning power?

10. **Skills.** Are you confident with your current professional and/or academic skillset, and the ability to leverage it accordingly to get what you want most out of life? Are you an expert at the things that are the core parts of your job and add the most value?

11. **Leadership.** How are you at leading yourself and others?

Additionally, how well do you lead functions or organizations? What about your influence and persuasion of those who don't report directly to you?

12. **Value.** What sort of value do you bring to your current workplace and/or school environment? Do you contribute to the growth and success of the company, your team, and your area? Or are you mostly doing busy work?

13. **Career.** What is your satisfaction level with your current job? If you're in school, what is your confidence level concerning your potential for satisfaction in future employment? How do you feel about the progress you're making toward the future? Do you feel in control of your career or are you relying on others?

Your Inputs

14. **Clarity.** How clear are you on what you need to do and why you're doing it? Do you have a direction for the future, or are you living day-to-day? Are you clear on what you need to do today and tomorrow?

15. **Action.** Do you often take action to accomplish your goals and objectives, or are you a heavy procrastinator? Are you a doer or a thinker? More importantly, are the actions you take the most important ones or are you busy being busy?

16. **Control.** Do you feel like you're in control of your own life? Are you intentional and proactive, or are you more reactive to what happens around you? Do you feel like a victim or a hero in control of your destiny?

17. **Boldness.** How much courage do you have? Do you get after it or do you worry about what could go wrong? Do you take occasional risks, or do you always play it safe?

18. **Emotional Intelligence.** How is your self-awareness, empathy towards others, motivation, self-regulation, and social skills?

19. **Excellence.** What standards do you set for yourself? Do you always strive to exceed your own expectations? How highly would you rate the quality of your work and actions?

20. **Extra.** Do you do the extra things that only a few people do? Do you give that little push beyond the basic needs? Are you extraordinary or ordinary?

Your Outputs

21. **Energy.** Everything in the universe is about energy. You can feel it all around you. How does your energy coming from the inside translate to the experience of you on others? Do you emit an overall positive energy or negative energy?

22. **Image.** How highly would you rate your personal brand? Think about a company brand. Are you trustworthy, unique, exceptional? How do others see and think about you if you were a corporate brand? Does your image reflect your core values?

23. **Influence.** How much can you influence someone else's thoughts and actions? Are you persuasive enough to get

people to think or take action? Or do you need authority to get someone to follow you?

24. **Impact.** What sort of impact do you have on the people, places, and things around you? How are others different because of you?

25. **Future.** Do you feel that your future is bright and filled with endless possibilities? Or do you feel that you have limited choices with outcomes that aren't as positive as you would like?

When you're done, notice which exercises you scored highest. Those are areas of strength in which you can build. Then, make a note of the exercises in which you scored the lowest. Pick three of them that matter most to you in terms of developing your best future self. Create an actionable plan for how you can work on these areas.

SELF-ASSESSMENT EXAMPLE

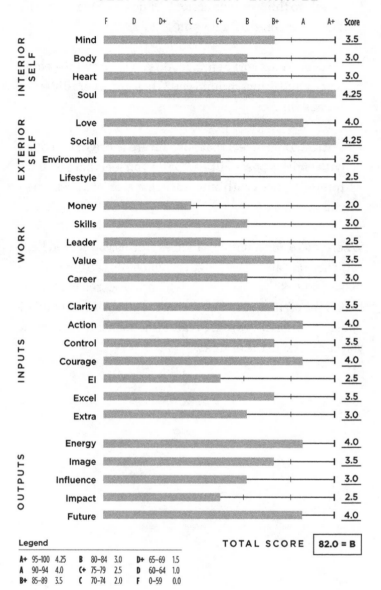

		F	D	D+	C	C+	B	B+	A	A+	Score
INTERIOR SELF	Mind										3.5
	Body										3.0
	Heart										3.0
	Soul										4.25
EXTERIOR SELF	Love										4.0
	Social										4.25
	Environment										2.5
	Lifestyle										2.5
WORK	Money										2.0
	Skills										3.0
	Leader										2.5
	Value										3.5
	Career										3.0
INPUTS	Clarity										3.5
	Action										4.0
	Control										3.5
	Courage										4.0
	EI										2.5
	Excel										3.5
	Extra										3.0
OUTPUTS	Energy										4.0
	Image										3.5
	Influence										3.0
	Impact										2.5
	Future										4.0

Legend

A+	95–100	4.25	B	80–84	3.0	D+	65–69	1.5
A	90–94	4.0	C+	75–79	2.5	D	60–64	1.0
B+	85–89	3.5	C	70–74	2.0	F	0–59	0.0

TOTAL SCORE | 82.0 = B |

Now, give the self-assessment to someone close to you and have them grade you on each exercise. Look at the areas where your scores for yourself differ from the scores someone else gives you. Those areas are where you need to research more and address why there are gaps in perceptions.

Once you've done the assessment, ask yourself what the most important things in life are to you, and what do you truly believe in and live by? These are your nonnegotiable core values that you will not deviate from and you must stand out for.

Top companies all over the world have a clear sense of their core values, and you should too. If they have a mission, vision, and core values, why don't you?

What else can you do to fully get to know you? Once you learn all about your likes and dislikes, what you're good at and not good at, who you are and who you want to be, what you want to do and not do, who you want to be around and not be around, that sense of clarity makes future decisions much easier.

Getting this clear vision of who you are is incredibly important because you'll need that origination point in your journey. Soon, you'll discover how this present self is pushed by your past and pulled into your future.

YOUR FUTURE SELF

An upcoming chapter dedicates much more time and detail to addressing your future. This smaller section concerns how you leverage your understanding of your past and present self to strive toward the person you want to become.

It's important to not only think about what you want to do but who you want to be. This section serves an awakening to your future self. Later on, you'll learn how to become much more familiar with that.

Start developing a clearer vision for your future self by understanding what's important to you now. Think about what makes you happy and what your core values are. Strive to live your version of happy and live to your core values each and every day going forward.

It's impossible to be someone else. Therefore, nobody else can be you. Be who you are and don't listen to anyone else who defines you. If you're truly honest with yourself and don't listen to what society thinks is best for you, you'll have a greater chance of success and happiness.

To further develop the idea of your future self, write a letter to that person. Describe who you are, what you're doing and how you feel. You can also create a resume that is you ten years from now and use that as a checklist and roadmap of what to do next. The point is to have an idea of your future, not someone else's vision of your future.

To truly stand out, you need to know how to align who you are today, which includes all the wonderfully unique skills and abilities you've always had, with how you'll become that better, future version of yourself.

Even if you never achieve that future version of your better self someday, that's okay, as long as you compete in the game of life, which is about the journey more than anything else.

Pursuing the things you love and staying true to your values is where you get most of life's fulfillment and satisfaction. Achieving your end goal is a tremendously satisfying feeling, but it's not everything. In fact, I would say the journey to get there is the most exciting and entertaining aspect of life.

The awareness of your future self has only just begun. In the next chapter, you'll learn much more about how to turn that vision of your better self into reality via purposeful self-reflection, a thorough understanding of what the world needs from you, and by taking to heart some words of wisdom from an important Japanese idea about your reason for being.

STAIRS TO HELP YOU BE THE REAL YOU

Today:

- Reflect on your past and list your previous successes, failures, and lessons learned.
- Perform a full present-day assessment via personality tests, SWOT analysis, etc.
- Form a vision of the future you; include lifestyle, type of job, ideal day, people around you.
- Develop your guiding principles, core values, and personal brand.
- Take as many self-assessments as you possibly can to get a full and rich picture of who you are and how others see you.

Every day:

- Reflect on yesterday and today to use what you learned and did for the next day.
- Think about today and what you need to do and focus on to be your best, truly live as you, and prepare for tomorrow.
- At the end of the day, determine if you acted as your true self and if you reflected your core values.
- Think about your tomorrow and plan ahead so you learn, grow, develop, and focus on what's most important to you and your future self.

Main goal: To achieve a deeper awareness and fuller understanding of your true self.

DEFINE YOUR FUTURE SUCCESS

3

"The best way to predict the future is to create it."

~PETER DRUCKER

As you develop the main character of your story, you decide where and how that character lives, travels, works, socializes, and more. You get to determine what the main character overcomes, what he or she accomplishes, and who that person is. Perhaps most importantly, however, you retain the power to create how the story ends for the main character.

By understanding who the main character is, how you want the story to be told, and how you want the story to end, you're free to determine the paths that may lead the character to his or her desired final destination. Keep in mind that limitless combinations of paths can lead to future success, and you can alter the course at any time.

PLAN ON IT

There is no singular pre-determined path to arrive at your future, but you must determine a destination and which path to take to get there. Plan wisely, however, because your journey will be an ongoing process consistently influenced by internal and external forces.

As long as you take the first step and continue moving forward each day, you'll be moving closer to where you want to be.

The worst thing you can do is wake up without a chosen destination and hope you magically land in your dream spot. As the children's fiction writer Lewis Carroll once said, "If you don't know where you're going, any road will get you there."

Let's say you're planning to take a vacation. If you already know you want to go to Cancun, that's great! No more thought is needed to determine your end point in that case. However, it's also helpful to just know that you want to go to a warm weather spot with a beach and have an idea of the certain activities you enjoy doing. You'll know generally what to pack, how to get there, and what to do once you arrive at your destination.

Isn't it interesting that we spend so much time planning and preparing to take a vacation, but we don't plan and truly prepare to take the ultimate trip, which is our own life?

At this point, you don't need to have a concrete determination of your future, but you need to make a plan with a general direction in mind. After all, you would never just show up at the airport without a bag packed and buy a ticket to some random destination in some random place. In fact, you likely don't leave the house without having a reason or knowing exactly where you need to go. Strangely, that's how most people approach life and their career.

Similarly, you don't have to find your one and only one true North Star. Life would be way too challenging and unfair if you have one and only one reason for being. Instead, your reason for being can be a fluid directional notion that could change over time. In fact, I would encourage you to build flexibility into your future plans. The more flexibility you have, the more opportunities you'll be presented with.

For example, if you have a singular focus on working for Disney in an operational leadership role, that's great. You'll need to be singularly focused on that one company in limited roles. But, if your reason for being is to work for a company that has the same values as you, offers a product or service that you love, and you can see the immediate impacts of what you do on other people, it opens an entire world of other amazing companies and roles that would fulfill your purpose in life.

A GPS FOR YOUR LIFE

To avoid wandering aimlessly with no clear destination or even a general direction in mind, I suggest using a GPS (Goal, Path, and Steps) for your life. Establish a goal, decide on a chosen path to get started, and take steps to move toward your current destination.

If you happen down the wrong path, allow your GPS to reroute you in a better direction. The ability to pivot while using that GPS is highly valuable. If you need to take a detour or choose a different goal or path, you should do so without regret or second-guessing.

Flexibility is a key ingredient. It's not often that things go exactly according to plan. With experience, knowledge, and other variables, you might decide to change your path. You could also take a step backward to enable two steps forward in a different direction.

Hopping from one path to another is completely acceptable and fairly certain in many situations. The only thing to avoid when defining your future success is standing still for too long.

FINDING YOUR IKIGAI

There are many ways to enter a chosen destination into your GPS for life. One way is to look to an ancient Japanese reason for being concept known as ikigai. This is your motivation for jumping out of bed and is thought to be the secret to a long, happy, and meaningful life.

In Japanese, the word, *iki,* means life or alive. The word, *gai,* means reflect, worth, or result. Your ikigai is at the center of four intersecting aspects of your life:

1. What you're good at (now or in the future).

2. What you love to do (something you would do even if you didn't get paid for it).

3. What the world needs from you (a problem to solve or something that makes life easier and better for others).

4. What you can get paid to do (after all, you need to support yourself and your family).

When you discover a career, passion, or activity that brings those four things together, you have found your ikigai—reason for being. If you only have a few of these four aspects in your job, you'll feel something missing.

Doing something you love and are good at will give you a sense of satisfaction and delight, but you might also feel the stress, concern, and uncertainty of not building enough wealth to live the way you want to.

Similarly, if you take a job that you're good at and can get paid for, but don't love it or find it has any meaning, you could experience emptiness and uselessness, which also won't make you happy.

Let's discover your life's intersection...

DISCOVER WHAT YOU'RE GREAT AT

People who stand out are great at something. More importantly, they're aware of their specific strength, and they market it and use it. Even better, some of them are great at two or more things that complement each other (like an analyst who is an expert modeler but can also tell the story behind the numbers, or a top basketball player who is also an excellent team leader). It's what they're known for and they do it better than anyone else.

Like most things in the game of life, the skills you're great at can change and develop over time. There may have been things in the past that you were amazing at, but as time passed, you might have forgotten, outgrown, or stopped enjoying them.

The reverse can happen as well. You may have struggled with some skills in the past but have become exceedingly talented at them today. Many skills in this world are only developed after substantial practice over a long period of time. Physiologically, our bodies and minds change, which means you may naturally get better or worse at a lot of things as you get older.

You should always try new things to see if you've overlooked something you could be great at in the future. Some people don't play golf until they're beyond the early development years, but from almost the first swing they take, it looks like they were pre-destined to patrol the fairways and greens of the world's most breathtaking and challenging courses.

Artists, musicians, business leaders, and most other professions are no exception. An in-born talent and skill could be untapped but deeply coded within your DNA, waiting to be released in all its glory. But they'll never burst onto the scene if you don't try them.

For example, I've always enjoyed helping people, which is why I'm writing this book, and I love giving keynote speeches. But there was a time when I wasn't necessarily a good presenter and as my story goes, I wasn't always the best student. Once I started to practice giving speeches and started speaking at colleges and universities, I noticed I enjoyed it a lot and made a concerted effort to continue to develop my presentation and speaking skills.

Now, I try to speak wherever I can about *The Standout Experience,* and I'm positively impacting people's lives with it. The past version of myself would have probably never understood this, but because I explored public speaking as an option, the future version of myself (now my present self) became adept at a skill I didn't think I had.

DISCOVER WHAT YOU LOVE TO DO

Coming to a full realization of what you love to do is a fairly intuitive process. You likely have a good idea of what these activities are already. Still, you might not be entirely sure.

To help you discover your love, ask yourself this question, "If I had a free day with no places to be, people to see, or to-do list to accomplish, what would I do with my time?" Or ask yourself what you would do for a living even if you didn't get paid for it?

I'm not recommending not getting paid, but for now, we're trying to determine what you love to do.

You might love hiking, reading, playing sports, going to church, playing video games, helping people, cooking, mountain climbing, etc. To come up with a complete answer to this exercise, you may also want to jot down some things you've never done before but want to try.

Think outside the box when exploring the many options available in this incredible existence. Have fun trying the full spectrum of pastimes the world has to offer. If you enjoy the kickstart of your heart from jumping out of an airplane or driving a motorcycle, go for it. If you prefer the serenity of being one-on-one with nature from gardening or walking in the woods, namaste.

DISCOVER WHAT THE WORLD NEEDS

There are so many unmet needs in the world today. Even if you're reading this fifty or one-hundred years from when it was written, I'll bet there are still plenty of things that people need on the Earth...or maybe it's Mars.

Think about other people's (or your) pain points.

What could be done better or differently?

What do people need to make their lives easier or better?

What could you offer that people don't realize they need until they see or do it?

What can bring immense joy, happiness, and excitement to people?

What problem can you solve, or what industry can you disrupt (Netflix, Uber, Airbnb, or Warby Parker)?

As a member of *The Standout Experience,* your challenge is to transform these unmet needs to opportunities in your mindset. Each of these provides a chance for you to have a game-changing impact in the world. Many of the top jobs today weren't in existence a few years ago.

Let's get back to the reality television dynamic for a moment. Think about the people who are successful on *Shark Tank.* They receive money and support from some of the world's most influential entrepreneurs and business leaders. What do most of the successful contestants have in common?

They address a specific gap of missing product or service in the world with a new idea that attempts to fill it. This could be by inventing an all-new device, or it could be by taking an existing idea and making it ten times better.

For now, assume you have no shortage of resources, like time, money, or anything else. Identify some pain points in the world. Write them down in your journal and make sure you can easily refer back to that page.

You may not have the answer to solve that area of need yet, but it may come to the future version of you. In that case, your future self will be glad that you had a good place to write down a brainstorming session and potentially create a solution to a big problem.

A key lesson I learned from one of my mentors is that the amount of success that you have is determined by the size of the problems you solve.

DISCOVER WHAT YOU CAN GET PAID TO DO

Be careful not to confuse the meaning of this aspect from the ikigai model. Discovering how to get paid to do something isn't for the sole purpose of making money. Rather, this is about getting paid to sustain life or to reinvest so you can grow whatever you're doing.

Many students and young professionals make the mistake of thinking exclusively about how to get paid for something. They might try to fill that need with something they're good at, which at least addresses two aspects of the ikigai formula for finding meaning. But they often disregard what they love doing, as if what they love and what they can get paid for are two opposing forces. They don't need to be. In fact, they shouldn't be.

People who make the mistake of considering what they love to do and how to get paid as opposites, often come to a stark realization later in life that they ignored contribution in their own fulfillment and happiness.

ALTERNATE APPROACHES TO DEFINING YOUR FUTURE

There are many other approaches to determining your future. The common denominator of all standouts is that they spend a lot of time thinking about their future, experimenting with different ideas, researching opportunities, meditating, and/

or talking to others. Then, they take the next steps, choose a destination, and start working towards it.

Your future needs to be a decision made with your heart, head, and soul. It's not enough to just want to do something. You have to be smart about it, have a reason for doing it, and be capable of being great at it.

The point is that Standouts make a choice, find a path to do it, and pursue their future with everything they have and with the right people around them. The ikigai model is only one way of helping you to do that. Here are a few alternate approaches for developing a future destination:

- **The Career Development Approach**—If your reason for being isn't yet known, choose a field you're truly interested in, and create a career learning and development plan in that respective field. Work on building a specific skill and expanding your network. You can also try different careers and fields while you're young. The goal is to explore and discover what you love. Just make sure your career isn't your only focus. The key is to have a life that you build a career around; not a career you try to build a life around.
- **The Dream Life-Goals Approach**—Focus on your long-term dreams and envision your ideal life with as much detail as possible. Then, build shorter-term SMART (Specific, Measurable, Achievable, Relevant, and Time-Based) goals to get there. Work your goals while tracking your progress to the idea you're targeting. The positive feelings you get from chasing your vision and achieving your goals one-by-one will push you into your future.
- **The Self-Expressive Approach**—Try working towards

who you want to be (not what you want to do). In this approach, your motivation and focus are to live as the full expression of your best self.

- Use the self-assessment exercise from Chapter 2 to discover your current weaknesses, and enjoy the personal growth that comes from getting better in those areas.
- Write down your ideal self so you are chasing a person that you want to be.
- Ask yourself these questions.
  - What are you passionate about? (If you had a day off today, what would you do?)
  - What great accomplishments of the past can you replicate in the future?
  - If your life had no limits, who would you be?
  - How do you want people to talk about you at your funeral?
  - Who do you admire most and would want to be exactly like (and why)?
  - What do you not like to do? (Sometimes knowing what to stay away from is a good way to understand what you want to do.)

- **The Full Exploration and Discovery Approach**—If none of that works, give yourself the freedom, flexibility, and permission to not know yet. Focus less on yourself and more on what the world has to offer. Approach each day with intention and a purpose to take risks, experiment, and enjoy the process of discovering your future. Expose yourself to as much as possible. Move forward as an innovative, discovery, and creative process to understand your destination at a later time. Unlike the career approach, this is the full exploration of everything in your life. Take the trips you want to take and meet the people you want to meet. Just make sure you take care of your basic financial and other needs as well.

Trusted external sources can also be tremendously helpful in your life planning process. The more questions you ask and the more people you talk to, the more you learn and get exposed to. You never know what one conversation or idea will spark an interest.

You can get help from your parents, teachers, mentors, bosses, coaches, and peers. But make sure you understand why they're giving you the advice they're giving.

Your parents might tell you to be an investment banker, a doctor, or an expert in data analytics. Ask yourself if they're really telling you to be those things specifically, or are they actually saying they want you to have a job that is in high-demand, has room for growth, and provides you with enough money to be safe, healthy, and happy?

Use all of your available resources. Keep trying, even if none of the advice seems helpful right away, because eventually, someone will provide a particularly impactful thought. Keep in mind, however, you should be cautious about asking for directions from people who have never been to where you're going.

YOUR FUTURE AND YOUR MOTIVATION

The key to making any of these approaches work lies in your motivation. Read Simon Sinek's book *Start with Why* or watch his Ted Talk. Standouts are both intrinsically and extrinsically motivated, but at their core, they know their why, what, and how.

More specifically, standouts...

- Know their purpose and mission (why).
- Live the appropriate lifestyle and take the appropriate actions (how).
- Get the results through the achievement of their goals (what).

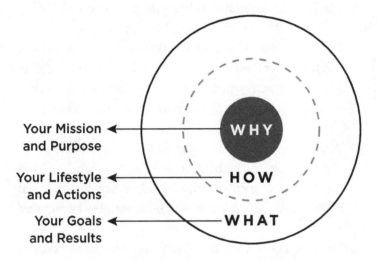

To be a standout, you need motivation to stick with your why, what, and how more consistently and over a longer period of time than the rest. There are other sources of motivation, but generally you're driven by one or more of the following:

1. **You get pushed by your past**—Previous success has the potential to breed more success, again and again. Similarly, a negative event can drive your will to overcome its consequences with just as much effectiveness. Many

people stand out in the minds of others because they overcame serious adversity. Therefore, your past can push you through victory and failure alike.

2. **You are pulled by your future**—A clear goal with a compelling why (reason) can inspire you to leverage your unique strengths and special abilities to accomplish great feats. This is a particularly powerful origin of motivation.

3. **You become uncomfortable with your present**—Many of us are attracted to change. It's natural to desire something better or wish for something different, but that's not where motivation comes from. Motivation from the present happens when you feel a burning deep inside you that *something must change* about your current situation.

4. **You become driven by the needs of someone else**— This is one of the highest forms of motivation. You have a spouse, a family member, a friend, or someone else who relies on you and needs you to be at your best every day.

5. **You just *love* something**—Whatever it is that you do, you can't wait to get up and do it again. It's something you always think about and would do it even if you didn't get paid for it. You're always trying to get better at it and want to be the best in the world. The enjoyment and fulfillment you get from doing this moves you to consistent action.

6. **You enjoy the discovery process**—By keeping an open mind, while moving in a positive direction towards something, you will discover motivation. With right intent and a desire to be better, you will undoubtedly find something

you love, something that moves you, and something you can't stop thinking about. You can also get a motivational high and a sense of inspiration from something you discover (or even create). This could actually be the sweetest origin for motivation of all.

7. **You crave organic chemicals**—Sometimes, we love to do things because of the feeling we get when we trigger chemicals in our bodies that impact motivation, productivity, and overall well-being. For example, by exercising, helping others, achieving a goal, or doing some other activity, you release chemicals that can inspire, help, or push you to do other things.

   A. **Dopamine**—Motivates us to take action. It reinforces pleasure when we achieve our goals.

   B. **Endorphins**—Released in response to pain or stress to provide relief. This is where people get a second wind or feel a runner's high.

   C. **Serotonin**—Moves throughout our body when we feel important or significant. Reflecting on past achievements or helping others boosts this chemical and makes us want to do more.

   D. **Oxytocin**—Creates trust and healthy relationships. This helps with creating strong bonds and improving social interactions, which is key to helping motivation as well.

   E. **Cortisol**—Essential for survival by helping us respond to impending danger. When we're put on high alert, motivation comes from the fear of what might happen and the urgency to do something to prevent it.

Many standouts I've talked to have a combination of driving forces working together in unison; the more they have, the more motivated they are. Some have all seven of those origins and when they do, watch out. When it comes to motivation, however, it only takes one to do amazing things in your own future!

GOALS ARE THE BRIDGE

Goals make up the critical bridge that takes you from where you are to where you want to go. Finding your Ikigai and defining your future is the all-important first step, but you then need to create a step-by-step action plan with clear goals, so you know how to get there.

These are your specific wayfinding points on the way to your destination. They tell you where to turn and when. Goals bring you back on course if you take a slight detour and motivate you to move from one waypoint to the next. They also help to break down your desired future that may seem too far away or unrealistic into simple and more manageable pieces.

As you accomplish each micro goal on your way to the macro target, you get the satisfaction of accomplishment and build momentum to reach the next one.

There are a lot of great ways to set goals, and you should find what works for you. I've included three great strategies that have worked for me to get you started on brainstorming some of your own.

1. Write your three to five dream future goals every day. Then, write one thing you will do to advance towards them.

2. Find different ways to stay motivated to work on those daily things, even when you don't feel like it.

3. Always assess where you are, how you're doing, and what's coming next. A good friend of mine, who is the CEO of Disney's credit union, shared his CEO Heat Map with me. This is what he uses to list his key strategic priorates, his end state goals, the steps that he needs to take to get him from here to there and a color-coded heat mapping system that highlights key micro goals or steps along the way that are high alert, areas of focus, next up and, already stable and completed. I think this is an example of an amazing tool to be used for your personal life as well as your business life.

PERSONAL HEAT MAP EXAMPLE

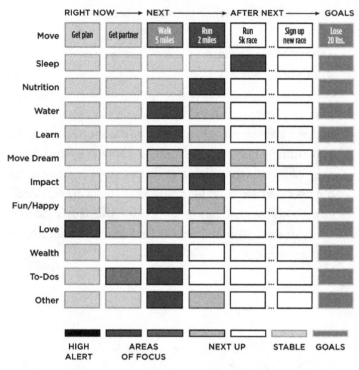

	RIGHT NOW ⟶		NEXT ⟶		AFTER NEXT ⟶		GOALS
Move	Get plan	Get partner	Walk 5 miles	Run 2 miles	Run 5k race	Sign up new race	Lose 20 lbs.
Sleep							
Nutrition							
Water							
Learn							
Move Dream							
Impact							
Fun/Happy							
Love							
Wealth							
To-Dos							
Other							

HIGH ALERT   AREAS OF FOCUS   NEXT UP   STABLE   GOALS

This is illustrative only. The number of columns, rows, and boxes, plus the row headers and goals, will vary based on the reader's particular needs.

Standouts live by the notion that taking daily action is life's greatest separator. They just do it! Here, the good become the great and the great become the standouts.

FOUR SUCCESS-DEFINED TAKEAWAYS

Ideally, you should walk away from this chapter with four key takeaways.

1. **Have a destination.** It doesn't need to be an exact pinpoint location, but you need to have a general direction in mind of where you want to go.

2. **Make sure certain basic necessities are met.** For example, suppose you discover that your future success lies in photography. Therefore, you begin to travel the life path of a photographer. You must also ensure that the basic elements of the previous self-assessment grades are met to a satisfactory level. In other words, your body, mind, and soul, as well as finances and family life must be in order. It won't do any good if you're the world's most successful photographer but can't pay your bills or meet your basic needs.

3. **Stay motivated.** Life is challenging and you won't always feel like moving towards your future. To embrace the challenge and keep moving forward, you need to find and use what motivates you. You also need to have goals, reward yourself for achievements, and make better choices to reach your goals. Remember to always choose what you want most versus what you want right now.

4. **Have fun!** Picking a direction is great and ensuring your basic needs are met is also important, but so is having fun. Life was not meant to just exist; it's meant to enjoy! The next chapter dives into this concept a little more deeply. In it, you'll begin to realize a complete transformation in your perspective on life. You're about to learn how to live life as the fun, challenging, and extremely rewarding game it really is.

Your future, success, and happiness are worth identifying and pursuing with everything you have. What will happen and how will you feel if you never give your goals and dreams a shot?

STAIRS TO HELP YOU DEFINE YOUR SUCCESS

Today:

- Create a future vision including your ikigai, top ten unreasonable life accomplishments, your definition statement of success, a vision board, a bucket list, eulogy statement, and any other forward-looking vision that inspires you.
- Decide what it will take, who you need to be, and who you need help from to make that future vision a reality. What would it feel like to be that vision?
- Set SMART goals and form a detailed strategic plan to get to your vision (monthly, quarterly, one year, three years, five years, and ten years from now). What KPIs (Key Performance Indicators) will you measure yourself against, and how will you reward yourself or celebrate the micro-wins on your way to greatness?
- Make sure you focus on holistic success. Don't put all of your energy into one thing, and don't make it about money or titles. You can't do it all, but you can ensure you don't have weak points that will negatively impact other areas of your life. Focus on what matters most to you.

Every day:

- Before the day starts, list one thing you will do to advance toward your key three to five goals.
- Create a daily checklist to track your progress and momentum towards your goals. Check each day to make sure you exercise, read a book, work on a key project, and see how many days in a row you can do it.
- Block the time (preferably early in the day) to work on the key project you need to work on that day.

- At the end of the day, check how you did against the day's strategic plan and share your successes with someone else. What can you do better tomorrow?

Main goal: Develop a grand vision of yourself and plan for your future.

PART 2

SIMPLICITY

"Simplicity boils down to two steps. Identify the essential. Eliminate the rest."

~LEO BABAUTA

PLAY THE GAME

"The game of life has two participants, spectators and players. Pick one."

~UNKNOWN

You may not realize it, but you've been participating for many years in one of the most exciting, engaging, and entertaining games ever created—the game of life.

It's important to realize that no test, interview, date, or any other seemingly *life or death* situation you might be encountering right now is actually life or death. They're normal day-to-day situations. If they don't go as well as you had hoped, the sun will come up tomorrow, and this wonderful game will present you with plenty of additional opportunities to play well and enjoy extraordinary success.

Life and death situations are about survival. Those situations concern things like food, shelter, and physical health. Life and death is not getting a good grade on a final exam, impressing a decision-maker on a job interview, or exhibiting irresistible charm on a first date.

Thinking about these moments as integral to your survival not only sounds ridiculous when you really think about it, but it also adds pressure and the unrealistic need for perfection. Rather, if you approach life as a game, these moments become fun and challenging (in a good way).

Life and death situations are about the fight or flight response in the moment. The good news is that you don't have to figure out life right now. If you're in your teens, twenties, or even your thirties, it's way too early in the game to stress about your career and what you're going to do with your life. In football terms, you just received the opening kickoff, and you're somewhere between the twenty- and thirty-yard line. There is a lot of playing field left to go, many first downs to make, and plenty of plays to execute.

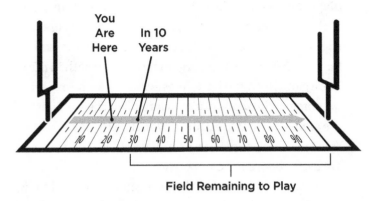

Field Remaining to Play

If you're further down the field of life and you want to start over, you can receive a punt, start a new offensive possession, and move down the field again to score your touchdown.

Standouts approach life and each situation as a game. This coincides with a scientific fact concerning the human brain. Our minds crave the benefits associated with competition and gaming. We love to have fun, and the rewards and recognition we get from achieving incentives through well-executed gameplay are real. They produce a release of dopamine that courses through our grey matter and produces an output of emotional highs. Life is like any other game that feeds our competitive spirit in that way.

THE TRUTH ABOUT GAMES

Life is so much better (and a lot more fun) if you approach

everything like it's a game, but keep in mind the following list of truths about all games.

- If you want to win, you need to know what game you're playing, as well as the rules and objectives. If the game is chess, you don't want to approach it like checkers. You should know exactly what success in this game looks like for you. Every situation, organization, and path in life is like a game. They all have rules, strategies, and expected outcomes. The more you're aware of all the elements of the game, the better equipped you'll be to play it.
- You can't always be the most talented player, but you can always outwork the competition.
- To compete at the highest level possible, you need to rigorously practice and prepare. As retired US Navy officer, SEAL commander, and Vietnam War veteran Richard Marcinko once said, "The more you sweat in training, the less you bleed in combat."
- The best strategy is to focus on being better than you were yesterday, sticking to a game plan, and having the resiliency and agility to pivot quickly as game situations require.
- Everybody wants to win, but the will to win and the belief that you will win leads to more positive outcomes.
- Winning is fun, but the most enjoyment comes from playing the game and giving more than your best.
- Playing a game requires teamwork and if it's an individual sport, it requires a team around you to be successful.
- Playing games involves social interactions that hone a variety of skills to help us succeed in life.

YOUR LIFE AS A GAME

As a young adult, you're about to enter one of the most interesting phases of the game; one where you'll be presented with numerous opportunities to play, many ways of playing, and many pathways to take; all of which will provide incredible opportunities to achieve sensational successes or occasional, brief failures.

Whether you win, lose, or draw at each opportunity, it's paramount that you continue driving forward. Don't sit still for too long or pass your turn to another player, because you only get one chance to play this game. Therefore, there's no point in taking a passive approach or letting other players zoom past you. It only makes sense to take as many actions as you can. Without a doubt, the best way to win at this game is to play with wild enthusiasm, never-ending hope, and heartfelt joy.

At this current stage of your life, you're making decisions that seem like do or die moments, but they're not. There is no one job or one major that provides a singular determining factor of absolute success or total failure.

It's not as if your entire lifetime comes down to one class that you can take with a pass/fail option. Winning at the game of life comes down to a much more cumulative process than any singular event can provide.

Often times, losing can be an incredibly useful outcome. You'll often find that a loss or failure becomes a blessing later. Your choices or life itself can actually be redirecting you to something better, although you might not realize it at the time. Have faith that one day you will look back and be thankful that you didn't win in that moment.

You also learn more from failures than successes. If you fail a big test at school, whiff on some key questions in a job interview, or crumble under the pressure of making a great impression on a first date, you can vow to not repeat those mistakes that led to the unfavorable outcome. In that sense, losing is a valuable lesson learned.

You can look at failure or loss as an experience to leverage to produce better outcomes in future opportunities. Sometimes, even the best generals need to lose a battle or two before they can win the war.

After a failure, you will get another turn. You can use that time to adjust a strategy. Players make good and bad plays in every game. It's important to adjust to the circumstances around you. That will eventually result in a winning strategy to the entire game.

The better you learn how to play this game, the happier, more fulfilled, and better off you and everyone around you will become. One outstanding moment can lead to another, and each of them can bring new hope. To truly play this game of life well enough to experience those victories, however, you'll need to know the rules, contents, objective, how to get started, how to play, and of course...how to win!

RULES OF THE GAME

Every game has rules and it's important to be aware of them, but let's be clear about one thing in particular. This book is about standing out, which means not following the normal societal rules that you and millions of other students and young professionals are being taught. I encourage you to break free from any limitations imposed by the mainstream about "do or die" moments and instead focus on separating yourself from the herd as exceptional.

Rules help everyone to play fairly and attempt to level the playing field. They determine the boundaries and a code of conduct by which to play. Rules instruct us how to move, how to keep score, what the penalties are, and how to win.

Some rules are very clear for a reason. They prevent injuries and keep us within certain limits that are unique to the game. Some rules are more ambiguous because while they're important, they also allow for a certain level of playability that makes the game fun. Some rules such as honesty, fair competition, and respect are unwritten, but we know to respect them appropriately.

To play any game, you have to know the rules. The more aware you are, the more you know which rules must be adhered to and which can be bent or even broken on occasion.

GAME CONTENTS

The game of life includes a unique board or playing field in which you get to perform and enjoy the game. It includes unique playing pieces that you have complete control over. You control what moves you make, what moves you don't make, and how you react when a move affects your game plan.

It's important to accept that life—like any other game— involves a small amount of luck and unpredictability, especially at the starting point. Although luck and unpredictability are two unchangeable realities that exist, you can do nothing about them, and strategy plays a much larger role in achieving the desired outcome. Also, the more you work and prepare, the more luck you seem to have.

Despite whatever perceived bad luck life throws your way, you always have the ability to maneuver your playing piece and make choices that allow you to ultimately become whatever you aspire to, as an adult. Cognitive thought, making choices, and having the ability to act on those choices is what makes us human.

THE GAMEBOARD

- **Your environment.** Your genetic makeup, where you were born, and the conditions you were brought into are preexisting elements of your environment. This represents the game board on which you are playing. You can't control these game components, but you can control how you play them, and you get to choose what game you play and where. The best players aren't the people who are simply given an advantageous starting point. They're the ones who know how to deal with a bad start, ride out the highs and lows of the game, and move their playing piece with precision to achieve success.
- **Easy versus hard paths.** Pay close attention to the game board and always look ahead. What seems to be an easier and quicker path to victory may actually turn into a harder road later. Conversely, a more challenging path now could lead to an easier road ahead. We said before that everyone faces challenges. Sometimes those challenges come early and sometimes they come later. You get to choose each path you take. Remember, however,

that any challenge or obstacle comes with new knowledge, more experience, higher rewards (for overcoming the obstacles), and a stronger playing piece. Do what's hard now to make your life easier in the future.

- **Jumping spaces.** Sometimes you get to pick a card, roll the dice, or get bumped by an opponent to a new and unexpected place. The top players know how to use that bump to their advantage to achieve their desired outcome. What might seem like hard luck might in fact be the unexpected break you needed or didn't know you needed until later in the game. Remember, there isn't a quick-fix jump to victory. You might get a short-term bump to a new space, but never lose sight of the fact that you're in it to win it for as long as it takes.

PLAYING PIECES

- **The most critical element of the game.** The playing piece itself is you. Your movement will determine how you succeed or fail in various points of the game. Ultimately, the decisions and actions you make will determine whether you win or lose. Understanding this important element is everything. Better awareness leads to better choices, which leads to better results. If you know what your playing piece (you) is capable of, you're better equipped to leverage the full range of its capabilities to your advantage.

- **Embrace your human playing piece.** The ultimate playing piece is your humanity. Being human means that we have basic needs, cognitive thought, abilities, and a full range of emotions just like all playing pieces are inherently the same at some level. We aren't perfect and there isn't anything that you can do to avoid the ups and downs.

Being human means having certain capabilities and potential but also having certain limitations and inherent flaws. Sometimes, we're driven by our capabilities and desires. But sometimes we're impacted by our limitations and flaws. Being human is the one way in which we're all exactly alike.

- **Each playing piece is unique.** There are approximately eight billion people in the world. None of them have your exact genetic makeup and no one will ever travel the exact path that you will. By default, you are one in a billion-plus and therefore you are special and unique. Nobody in the history of the world has ever been you before, and no one will be you ever again. Accept that your uniqueness and what your playing piece can do is how you play and how you're going to stand out.

- **Types of playing pieces.** Thinkers, talkers, and doers are the three types of playing pieces in the game. All humans have the ability to think, communicate, and take action. You can think about something, and you can even talk about it, but neither accomplishes anything unless you take action. To stand out, you must be a doer. It's not enough, however, to take action just once. The impact of doing something consistently, hopefully every day, is far greater than what you do only once in a while. You can exercise once or diet for a day, but unless you do it consistently, you won't get healthy or have the physical appearance you desire.

- **Accept what your playing piece can and can't do.** Don't ever compare yourself to others or be jealous of what other players have or can do. They aren't you and they can't do what you can do. Instead, embrace your unique abilities. Use them to your advantage based on the game situation.

OBJECTIVES

You can't play any game well unless you know what you're trying to accomplish. Playing without clear objectives is like dribbling a soccer ball around an endless, boundaryless field with no goals. It might be fun for a few minutes, but you'll lose interest quickly.

- **Enjoy playing.** Having fun is the most important facet of this game. Life is serious, but it's also wonderous, enjoyable, and full of possibilities. You can't have long-term success if you aren't happy in what you are doing. The best of the best enjoys playing the game so much that practice doesn't feel like practice. They see it as a way to get better. Tough games and losses aren't the end of the world. Competing and learning from them are the small victory within those experiences. Playing for others is enjoyable for the best of the best, and they feed off that energy. They enjoy the game so much, they would play it in an empty parking lot at midnight with no one watching.
- **Play strategically.** To play any game, you have to know what you're trying to accomplish and where you're trying to go. To play this game well, your singular goals and larger objectives require clarity. You can't approach the game randomly or without purpose. Think deeply about your strategy and plan carefully how you'll get there. Give yourself the flexibility to alter your strategy and change course as needed but keep your focus on how you'll win.
- **Winning itself.** Winning is determined by one thing only...you. You need to determine what success and happiness is for you. Play the game your way, and make sure that your success is your success, not someone else's definition of success.
- **The next challenge.** Even when you win a game or a

championship, there is always the next thing, another level, and a new challenge. Standouts always find a way to focus on the next opportunity. When they reach the pinnacle, they create a new future for the way the game is played. They also set a higher bar for others to reach. This may sound strange, but they never feel like they've won anything. Instead, they accomplish that particular goal or level and maintain a burning desire to see what comes next. If there are no more challenges, help someone else win.

GETTING STARTED

- **Everything you need is available.** There is a limitless stockpile of resources to help you play this game. You can get information in an instant through a handheld electronic device. There are no shortages of people who can help you...mentors, friends, family members, teachers, leaders, coworkers, and others. You can earn money through a variety of ways. You can acquire almost any skill, many for free on the internet. There is an abundance of resources to help you, but you must know where to look and take the necessary action to capitalize on them.

- **Take the first step.** Perhaps, you've heard the quote, "You don't have to be great to start but you have to start to be great." Maybe you've also heard, "The journey of a thousand miles begins with the first step." Both of those pieces of wisdom apply well to the game of life. Once you've determined your end target, you need to start moving. This might be the hardest part. Many players wait for the right moment because they don't want to fail or be seen as incompetent. That's the ego talking. Everyone who accomplished anything great started as a beginner. You'll face a lot of resistance internally and externally. It's hard to start anything, whether you're attempting to begin exercising, getting a new job, or acquiring a new skill. Everything is working against you—the weight of change, the pressure to see immediate results, and the resistance to keep moving forward. As you start to build momentum, however, it gets easier. What you struggle with now will pay tremendous dividends later.

- **Create momentum.** The start is always the hardest, but once you build one move on top of another, you create momentum and each move becomes easier. Anyone who has played any game knows that if you come out swinging from the start, you can build momentum that helps you take control of the game. You get to play offense and make others catch you. At key moments, you can also change the momentum, which can often determine the outcome. Momentum is an extremely powerful force, and when you lose it, it can be difficult to get going again.

GAMEPLAY

- **Always be moving forward.** Once you get started, don't move just for the sake of moving, but continue making strategic actions that propel you forward. You can't win by standing still. Nothing in this game comes to you. You must go to it. Life is constantly evolving. If you stay still, opportunities will pass you by. If you get knocked down seven times, make sure you get up eight. If you run into a wall, find a way to go around it, over it, or through it, if necessary. Passivity is not a recommended strategy in this game, because it will only result in more active players catapulting themselves ahead of you. To compete, you'll need to take action early and often. Besides, waiting around gets boring.

- **Expend your energy wisely.** There is an interconnectedness between the universe and all living things. We all have an energy that should be used conscientiously because it affects not only ourselves, but the people around us as well. Your inputs determine your outputs and your outputs are someone else's inputs. Know how to build your energy, store it, and use it at the right moment. Be conscious of how your energy impacts others. Energy is one of your most precious resources and very few know how to use it wisely.

- **Accept that it will be hard.** The greatest joys usually come from the most difficult goals. Anything that comes easy is taken for granted and the good feeling wears off quickly. Embrace the struggle and the challenge that comes with having a worthy goal. If you spend your energy trying to avoid challenges, you won't have the energy, time, or focus needed to actually play the game well. In that case, you'll be playing a game that minimizes the bad instead of enjoying the good. If you do what's hard now, the game will become easy. However, if you do what's easy now, the game will become harder.

- **Competition is everywhere.** Compete every day, not just with others but also with yourself. We all have desires, wants, and needs, and we must compete fiercely to get them. Do not let other players attempt to manipulate your free will. Everything that happens in your life is ultimately your responsibility. The successes are yours to celebrate and the failures are yours to learn from. There's no point in having the mindset of a victim. If you don't get the results you hoped for from a job interview, accept responsibility for it. You weren't shortchanged or the victim of a bad break. There is always something you can do better. Even better than competing? Try dominating!

- **Direction matters.** Life is full of decisions, all leading to certain paths with outcomes at the end of each journey. If you feel like you're heading down the wrong path, it's never too late to pivot to a different one but keep moving forward. Like a train that comes to a rail switch or a plane that reaches a waypoint, even the slightest degree of change can make that train or plane reach a completely different destination. Be intentional with the direction of each step and keep moving forward. The more steps you take in the right direction, the better you'll play the game.

- **Proactive and reactive moves.** Sometimes, your movement will be based on a proactive choice you've made, as a smart way of preparing for a future challenge or opportunity. Other moments, you'll be forced into a reactive state, which is fine, but remember to not let those reactive decisions dictate where you go. Instead, take in the external force that impacted you, think about what you're trying to accomplish (long term), adjust your strategy, and continue moving forward. The more you control the game, own the game, and make others play to your strengths and style, the easier it will be to win.

- **Pain and loss are unavoidable.** You will occasionally experience pain, losses, and setbacks. It's an unavoidable aspect of our humanity. Do your best to minimize pain when it happens and appropriately to bounce back. Then, use that setback to get better and add fuel to your drive to win.

- **Change is unavoidable.** Even if you don't ever want to change, the human body is always changing. The eight billion people around you grow and change, as well as the environment. The economy changes, as well as businesses and customers. Change is a constant in this game, and there is nothing you can do about it. The players who fight change lose. Meanwhile, the people who embrace change and use it to their advantage become better and win.

- **Hard work and preparation are required.** Hard work is a basic requirement of this game. It gets you a seat at the game table and gives you a chance to compete, but much more will be required, such as a positive attitude, a winning strategy, and a clear vision of what success will look like for you.

WINNING

- **Success is a holistic concept.** Winning the game is dependent upon successes across multiple dimensions. Contrary to the famous tongue-in-cheek saying, whoever dies with the most money or toys does not win. Winners succeed in many areas of life because excelling in one area impacts others. Winning is dependent on your individual version of success, which includes your terms, across multiple dimensions. It's comforting to have money and a good job, but you also need to feel safe, be happy and healthy, learn, grow, have great people around you, have a positive impact on others, and any number of other factors that contribute to your vision of what winning the game ultimately looks like. Don't focus on only one aspect of success. That's winning a battle but not necessarily the war.
- **Success looks different for everybody.** Your version of success is different than others'. This is your game. You determine the paths you take, what winning will look like,

and the ultimate outcome. At the end of your lifetime, loss equates to the gap between what you accomplished and what you really wanted, which creates regret. But loss is never how you didn't measure up to someone else's success or someone else's expectations.

- **You have to be different.** Your genetic makeup is different from everybody else's. If you try to conform to what someone else is doing, you won't be able to duplicate their success because you don't have their specific set of skills. However, they don't have your specific set of skills. To stand out, you need to leverage all the best qualities that make you different. The more effectively you do so, the more you'll increase your chances to win the game!

ADVANCED GAMEPLAY

To stand out means you play the game with a special *X-factor* that stirs the minds, hearts, and souls of others. It also means you prepare to overcome challenges when it matters most, you end up being a game changer and set the bar higher for the next player. You stand out by being in control of the game, rather than the game controlling you. Perhaps most importantly, you learn how to get better from one game to the next.

This chapter has provided a basic guideline for how to think about the game and offers some strategies for playing it well. By approaching every day and each situation as a game, understanding the rules, having a strategy, and competing to win, while enjoying the moment, you'll stand out.

If you continue to put pressure on yourself, focus on what could go wrong, and live reactively, competing will be much more difficult, and winning will be almost impossible. So, why live that way? Remove the pressure by living like you're playing a game! If you enjoy playing, you've already won, no matter what the outcome might be.

STAIRS TO HELP YOU PLAY THE GAME

Today:

- Be clear on the game objectives. How do you win and what does success look like? What rules can you bend, break, or create as new, and which rules must you follow?
- Understand the type of player you are (offensive, defensive, or a mix of both). Are you a risk-taker or are you risk-averse? Do you go all in or are you more cautious? How do you prepare and practice for game day and when are your important game days?
- How do you respond to challenges or key game situations? How can you rise to a level that others can't match?
- Why do you need to win and what will it feel like when you do? How do you improve for the next game or the next season?

Every day:

- Discover whether or not you won the day. If you feel like you lost today, what did you learn and how can you capitalize on that for next time?
- Assess if your new self was better today than your old self would have been. Did you compete at your highest level?
- Reflect on the ways you helped your teammates. Were they better because of your input? Did you set a standout example for other players?

- Did you embrace today's challenges, enjoy the competition, and have fun playing the game? If not, why?
- How were you a game-changer today?

Main goal: Reframe your life as a game and understand what type of player you are.

**LIVE HAPPY,
LOVE DEEPLY!**

5

"Success is not the key to happiness. Happiness is the key to success."

~ALBERT SCHWEITZER

Money, titles, fame, big houses, and fancy cars are examples of societal measures that supposedly determine happiness. At least that is what we're led to believe. What if it works in reverse? What if being happy is a key factor in determining your wealth, fame, title, the things you have, and all the other measures by which society determines success?

Years of research has shown that happiness directly impacts health, how long you live, the quality of your relationships, and your emotional well-being. The memories of earlier happy feelings also provide a sense for how you're living. It also helps you to determine if you've led a good life or a bad life to this point.

It's also true that happiness doesn't just happen to you. You create your own happiness, which then works *for* you.

By investing your time, energy, and resources in doing the things you like to do, working on your growth and development, surrounding yourself with the right environment, touching your five senses in a positive way, and doing other things that foster happiness, you create a positive emotional feeling. Research has shown that positive feelings lead people to work more actively on the things that matter, which then builds success.

When you're happy, you also feel optimistic, energetic, and more confident. Others sense those feelings and become drawn to you in a positive way. It's a beautiful circular reference that starts with you, knowing who you are, and where you're going.

Unfortunately, it takes some people years of experience and acquired wisdom to figure out how to be happy. Still others focus so much on the wrong things and never figure it out for themselves. Think about how many famous people live with an abundance of fame and fortune. Outward appearances make them seem to have it all, but in reality, many of them live with debilitating loneliness and unhappiness on the inside.

Some people including the ones that truly stand out in life, discover early on what it means to be happy. They experience new things and learn what they like and don't like. Then, they double down on those lessons learned. They discover that happiness comes from connecting with others, appreciating the little things, and having an impact on the world.

Bronnie Ware is a palliative care nurse and author. She spent many years caring for patients in the last few months of their lives. During that time, she had many heartfelt experiences while talking to them and learning about their regrets in life. She wrote a memoir about the experience called *The Top Five Regrets of the Dying*. Her research led to five surprising results about the patients.

1. They all wish they'd had the courage to live their own life, not the one that others wanted or expected them to live.

2. They wish they hadn't worked so hard and spent more time with family.

3. They wish they would have expressed their true feelings to others more often.

4. They wish they had stayed connected with their friends (deep connection is the most powerful of our human interactions).

5. They wish they had allowed themselves to live happier.

Notice that none of these regrets involve money, titles, status symbols, or society's success expectations. If you've ever been to a funeral and talked to the family and friends of the loved one they are remembering and celebrating, you never hear them talk about the jobs they had, the money they earned, or the fame they received. They talk about the type of person they were, the life they lived, and the impact they had on others.

Stuart Scott was a charismatic and impactful anchor of ESPN's SportsCenter program. As he battled cancer, he talked about beating the disease and living your measure of success "by how you live, why you live, and in the manner in which you live."

Years earlier, at ESPN's ESPY awards show, Jimmy Valvano (who was also battling cancer) said defiantly, "Cancer can take away all of my physical abilities. It cannot touch my mind. It cannot touch my heart, and it cannot touch my soul. Those three things will live on forever."

Earlier in the speech, he said, "To me, there are three things we should do every day. Number one is laugh. You should laugh every day. Number two is think. You should spend some time in thought. Number three is, you should have your emotions moved to tears. If you laugh, think, and cry, that's a full day. That's a heck of a day."

Gretchen Rubin wrote an amazing book titled *The Happiness Project*. I followed her year-long program on happiness, which included a different happiness topic each month. That book and program provided tremendous insight into how and why I was happy at various times in my life. I applied that experience, along with the research from other experts to shape my beliefs on the subject and discover new ways to be happy.

All of these people, from the dying to the living, can't be wrong. Happiness is letting go of what you think your life is supposed to be like and not focusing on the things that others think make you happy and successful. As Christian Dior said, "Happiness is the secret to all beauty. There is no beauty without happiness." Happiness is also the secret to standing out.

THE FOUNDATIONS OF HAPPINESS

Achieving a lifetime of happiness means learning to master individual moments within each hour of every day. Experience enough great moments within a twenty-four-hour period and you'll have a great day. If you put enough happy days together, you'll have a happy week. Enough happy weeks lead to happy months, and happy months lead to a happy year. Live enough happy years and you'll have a happy life. Success will naturally follow.

Unfortunately, many in the world today aren't happy. Looking at the annual World Happiness Report (yes, there is such a thing), the General Social Survey, or the latest Harris Polls, reveal that many people are the unhappiest they've been in years and the trend is heading downward. More specifically, a recent Gallup poll showed that more than half of all Americans are unhappy in their current jobs.

Standing out involves not only knowing when the right opportunity happens and how to capitalize on it, but also having an internal feeling of peace, happiness, and enjoyment that allows you to live fully and perform in the moment. Standing out also means you radiate happiness, positivity, and energy, while the rest of the world focuses on what's going wrong.

If you reflect on why someone stood out to you in the past, you'll likely recall a positive output of energy they gave you.

As you learned earlier, the most important thing to know about happiness is that it doesn't come to you. If you wait for someone else to make you happy, you're giving away your power and putting your faith in something in which you have no control.

You must create your own happiness. Once you do that, your output becomes a powerfully positive energy, which becomes input for others who interact with you. Those inputs then affect their outputs as the beautiful circle of human connectedness continues.

The question then becomes, how do you create your happiness that inspires that energized, positive flow of inputs and outputs among all of us throughout the world?

Through my own long and often difficult journey, I've learned that certain thoughts, actions, environments, and feelings can compound each other to create happiness.

Although I'm sure many more exist, I've listed twenty of these happiness-creating elements that have been learned from my own life and validated through so many amazing people, books, seminars, social media posts, coaching discussions and other wonderfully influential resources.

Challenge yourself to create happiness in as many ways as you can each day. The more you do and the more often you do them, the stronger your feeling of happiness will be in each day and throughout your lifetime.

CREATING HAPPINESS

1. **Protect your core and replenish your energy.** First and foremost, exercise regularly, sleep well, and eat right. Happiness comes from feeling well and being physically ready to tackle each day.

2. **Read or learn something new.** Your mind requires growth as a basic necessity. It craves knowledge, information, ideas, new thoughts, new experiences, and wisdom. The more you grow, the healthier your well-being will be, the more enjoyment you'll have, and the more optimism you will feel.

3. **Take control of your day.** If you don't own your day, someone else will and you will live out that person's happiness. To achieve your version of happiness, be in control of your day either through your actions or how

you think and feel. The more positive intentions you implement, the more you'll feel your own version of happiness.

4. **Be kind and help others.** We're built to ensure our survival, as well as that of the community around us. Commit random acts of kindness and help others in times of need whenever possible. Contributing to someone else's happiness or success is an extremely rewarding feeling.

5. **Focus on TLC (Time, Love, and Connection).** Our close relationships and a strong sense of connectedness with others is one of the deepest of all human needs. Make connecting with others your highest priority. When you share your time, love, and connection with others, you give them the greatest gift of all. People don't want your material presents. They crave your undistracted and connecting presence.

6. **Contribute and add value.** We all want our lives to have meaning. Your happiness is directly correlated to the amount of value you bring to your job, to your day, and to others. The more you contribute meaningfully in the day, the more gratitude and satisfaction you will feel throughout your lifetime.

7. **Feel productive.** The feeling of accomplishment is palpable and the more you do, the better you'll feel. Cross off important tasks on your to-do list (don't be busy being busy). Tackle the next micro goal on your way to a macro goal and advance on a key project. The feeling of individual accomplishments is tremendously rewarding, and it can stick with you all day.

8. **Practice gratitude**. Develop an appreciation for the people, places, and things that surround you in the game of life. Journal your thoughts and refer back to them in moments of sadness. Plenty of things to be grateful for exist around all of us. Scientific research has consistently proven the immense power of gratitude every day, so practice it with conviction.

9. **Anticipate the future**. A positive outlook has the power to create happiness. Knowing the reward at the end of the day, week, or even month creates a sense of excitement and anticipation that can contribute to your happiness every day. Remind yourself of the opportunities for fun that are ahead of you. If you don't have anything like that on the horizon, plan a vacation, sign up for a race, make dinner reservations, call a friend to get together for drinks, or get the wheels in motion for some other experience to get excited about.

10. **Use your past**. Your past can be something that pulls you down or it can be something that lifts you up. Many of your greatest accomplishments and a deep sense of enjoyment can be generated by overcoming undesirable outcomes from your past. You can also relive the same happy moments over and over again.

11. **Get clarity.** With increased clarity you gain greater control, which enables you to be more prepared and tuned into the opportunities and challenges of each day. Consequently, a lack of clarity creates confusion, frustration, and chaos.

12. **Consume something motivational or inspiring.** Con-

sider how listening to upbeat music or watching an inspiring movie can make you feel. The motivation you get from specific sources can give you the confidence, power, and energy to create happiness. Particularly inspiring selections have the power to make you feel like you can take on the world. Rather than allowing those moments to come and go, act on them. After experiencing them, do something positive to create happiness that carries well beyond the moment.

13. **Solve a problem.** Ever notice that when you hear a problem, you shift right into problem-solve mode? It's human nature to want to solve problems, find creative solutions, help others, and make things better. Solve and evolve. Tackle a problem or something challenging to create a feeling of happiness in yourself and/or others.

14. **Close the gap between your expectations, wants, and desires, and what you actually do.** The greater the congruence between what you want and what you do, the happier you'll be. Dissatisfaction comes from when you do something you don't want to do or is misaligned with your values and happiness. Find more things that align with your desires and dreams.

15. **Feel secure.** Taking from Maslow's Hierarchy of Needs, the more your physiological needs—security, belonging, esteem, and self-actualization—are met, the happier (and more motivated) you will become. Having these needs met provides a level of comfort, safety, and security that allows you to focus on the next level of needs. It's impossible to be happy if your basic needs aren't met.

16. **Do something new.** Variety is indeed the spice of life. We all get a lift from new experiences, people, and ideas. The more new things you do, the less mundane your day is and the happier you will feel. Sometimes, this is as simple as taking a new route to work. Experiment with numerous ways to break from the same old, same old.

17. **Think positively.** How you think determines how you feel. What you take in and assign meaning to, determines how you think. Watch your inputs and train yourself to enjoy the victories or take the lesson from failures. Either way, enjoy the challenge.

18. **Do whatever makes you happy and remove what doesn't.** Building time into your day to foster happiness needs to be a priority. Sound simple enough? You might be surprised at how many people don't proactively make this a crucial part of their day. My advice is to get out and enjoy life. Take in more of the things that make you feel alive. You can also create happiness through subtraction (eliminating unhappiness). Get out of toxic relationships. Remove yourself from unproductive environments and walk away from the things that you dread waking up in the morning to do. This could very well involve leaving your job or something else that's equally undesirable. Life is too short to do the things that make you unhappy.

19. **Move your emotions through your five senses.** Make sure you touch your own emotions by eating the foods you love, listening to the music that makes you feel upbeat, taking in the wonderful smells of nature, touching something that feels good, or taking in the beautiful

sights around you. The more positive experiences your five senses enjoy, the happier you'll feel.

20. **Harness the positive energy and love of others.** Being around people with positive energy makes you feel more positive and happier. In psychology, this is called social contagion, which is the affect or behavior one person has on another. It's why you feel happy when you're around someone else who is happy. Similarly, social contagion is also why you feel tense when you're around someone who is stressed. Most importantly, the quality of your relationships is a big determining factor of your happiness. Make sure you surround yourself with people who live life with you, love you, and make you happy. The most important decision you'll make for your happiness and success will be the person (spouse, partner, best friend) you spend the most time with.

Most importantly, find what makes you happy. It could be some, all, or none of the elements above but it might not. Your version of happiness is the only thing that matters. Don't leave your happiness in the hands of the world or other people. You get to live your own life and create your own happiness. Get to know what that is, how you do it, and how it makes you feel. Be intentional about incorporating that into your daily routine and make it your life's work. If you're happy, those around you will also be happy.

THE IMPACT OF LOVE

Love—particularly intimate love—is a powerful feeling and has been proven to be a strong predictor of health and happiness (which we know leads to success). However, the impact of love isn't restricted to the romantic notion.

Close relationships with children, parents, siblings, friends, and colleagues can also increase your level of happiness. Your interactions with these people and others, as well as the things you do, also represent forms of love that ultimately contribute to happiness. Love, in all its incarnations, is another secret to standing out.

Steve Jobs spoke many times about the importance of loving what you do. At a D5 Conference in 2007, he said that you need to love what you do because "it's so hard that if you don't (love it) any rational person would give up. It's really hard. And you have to do it over a sustained period of time. So, if you don't love it and you don't have fun doing it, you're going to give up. That's what happens to most people."

Feeling love can also provide an excellent source of motivation. It connects you with other people, it's the path to self-discovery, and it teaches you about life. Love gets you through tough times and it can be a powerful determining factor in your future.

The critical factor in all of this is that it requires your valuable resources (time, energy, and talents). The more you put into it, the more you will get out of it.

DEPOSITS AND WITHDRAWALS
Always Give More Than You Take

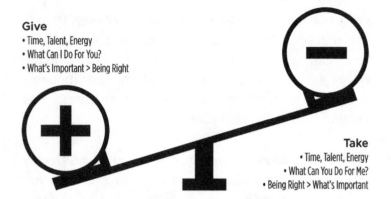

Give
- Time, Talent, Energy
- What Can I Do For You?
- What's Important > Being Right

Take
- Time, Talent, Energy
- What Can You Do For Me?
- Being Right > What's Important

Love is also a long-term play, feeling, and investment that pays long-term dividends. That's why any love expert will tell you to lose the battle (in a relationship, disagreement, business partnership, etc.) if necessary to win the war. The short term is temporary, but the long term can impact forever.

The bottom line is: to be successful, you must be happy. To be happy, you must have love in your life. To have love in your life, you must be true to who you are, hold high standards for the love around you, and put more into your love than you take out.

As Jobs also said, "You have to find what you love. And that is as true for your work as it is for your lovers. Your work is going to fill a large part of your life, and the only way to be truly satisfied is to do what you believe is great work. The only way to do great work is to love what you do. If you haven't found it yet, keep looking. Don't settle. As with all matters of the heart, you'll know when you find it. And, like any great relationship, it just gets better and better as the years roll on. So keep looking until you find it. Don't settle..."

A FINAL WORD ON HAPPINESS

Ultimately, happiness is whatever you decide it is. Because you're in control of your life, you're able to create your own happiness. Sometimes you might need help, and other times, happiness will unfortunately elude you. Those are certainties of this world.

Experience tells us that we can't be happy all the time. Life is complicated and always changing, so just like good times come and go, so will the occasional negative experience. We all have our own motivations, and everyone strives to be as happy as possible with whatever resources they have. Pay attention to those things that happen most often in your day. This includes your work, the people around you, your lifestyle, how much you travel, and all other inputs.

Happiness is different for everyone, and it can be a difficult thing to grasp. The challenging and endless pursuit of happiness is the most fun part of life, and that in itself, creates more happiness. Take in the beauty of the entire journey!

STAIRS TO HELP YOU LIVE HAPPY, LOVE DEEPLY

Today:

- What makes you feel alive and what is your ideal happy day (experiences, people, work, growth)?
- What have been your happiest moments so far and how can you do it again or make those a part of your every day?

- Since love is happiness and happiness is love, what are the things that you love to do and who is it that you truly love (and truly loves you)? What can you do to enhance, deepen, and grow the love in your life?
- Define your standards for living, loving, and being happy. What are you not going to tolerate (minimum standards) and what do you fully expect and deserve (highest standards)? Make sure everything and everyone in your life lives up to your standards.

Every day:

- How did you live today and how does it align with your ideal day?
- Reflect on what made you happy today and what you will do tomorrow to create happiness.
- Who did you show or give love to today? In your relationship, did you make more deposits in love than you took? As a leader, did you show love and care to your team and key partners? What did you do that you really loved doing?
- What and who lived up to your standards today? What and who didn't? How can you impact that result in a more positive direction tomorrow?
- Rate your day in terms of living, loving, and happiness. What can you do tomorrow to be more alive, more in love, and create more happiness?
- Main goal: Make happiness and love a priority in your life.

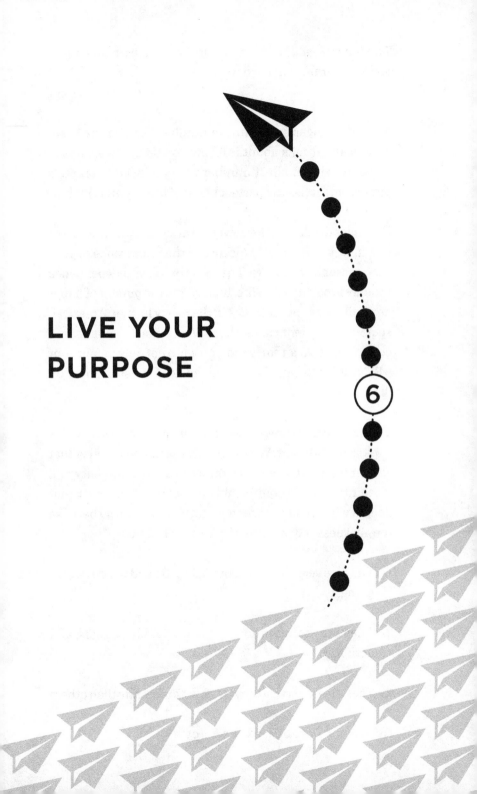

LIVE YOUR
PURPOSE

6

"Life is never made unbearable by circumstances but only by lack of meaning and purpose."

~VIKTOR FRANKEL

Amazing power exists in the number three. Your brain recalls and thinks about information better in groups of three. It's the smallest number that you need to create a pattern and it has the perfect blend of brevity and rhythm.

Examples displaying the power of three are everywhere. For instance, we previously discussed the importance of your past, present, and future. The Declaration of Independence proudly proclaims that life, liberty, and the pursuit of happiness will be essential values in the newly formed American society. In ancient times, there were friends, romans, and countrymen. At an early age, you were not only taught your ABCs and 123s but also to stop, look, and listen and stop, drop, and roll.

The instances of three are everywhere in this world and this book is no different. We've already discussed the idea that all humans need three basic things—clarity, simplicity, and certainty—to live comfortably and thrive. You know that people who stand out when it matters most do so because they harness the power of three core elements:

1. They are very clear about who they are and where they're going.

2. They break things down into simple ideas, goals, and action steps.

3. They create certainty by thinking differently than others,

doing things differently than others, and preparing differently than others.

The power of three becomes more evident over the next three chapters where we will focus on your purpose, journey, and foundations. More specifically, in this chapter, you'll learn all about how life's purpose is based on three core pillars.

With better awareness of this immense power of three, you will then live the power of three by making better choices, seeing better results, and more importantly, standing out from the rest.

REVEALING LIFE'S PURPOSE

One of the few certainties in life is that at some point in the future (if you haven't already), you will ask yourself some important questions.

- What is my purpose?
- What difference can I make in the world?
- In what ways will I be remembered?

Countless articles and books have already been written about purpose. Philosophers, spiritual leaders, psychologists, and bar room life advisors have been debating this thought-provoking question for centuries. We search for our own meaning and we admire people who seemingly found their specific purpose in life.

I've asked myself these same questions from the confusing, early years through my successful professional career, and well into my adulthood. I've tried to find purpose by reading books, attending conferences, and talking to family, friends, mentors, leaders, peers, and others.

Based on my personal experiences and the insights gained from many incredible people who stand out in their industry, company, team, or community, I learned to reshape how I think about purpose, and it's been a game changer for me. Instead of chasing that elusive singular thing that I was meant to do and feeling like it was a headwind holding me back, I have a new set of beliefs, which feels more like a strong and refreshing tailwind pushing me forward:

- We don't have a singular purpose in life, but we all have the same three reasons for being here.
- We don't *find* our purpose. Rather, we create a personal mission that aligns with the three reasons we're here.
- Your personal mission can and probably will change over time.
- You will eventually evaluate your life based on how you fulfill your three reasons for being here, but you'll remember and think back on your life based on the mission(s) you passionately pursue. This will also be how others remember you.

Let's first define and clarify the difference between purpose and a mission. Purpose is a reason for which something (or someone) is created or exists and it relates to a three-pillar purpose model I call Rise, Shine, and Impact. These three pillars, which I will explain soon in this chapter, constitute the three reasons we're all here. They represent our why.

From that purpose, we live fully by writing our own story

within that model, but we get to determine our own individualistic what and how. This is called our mission, which is a strongly felt aim, ambition, or calling. This represents your what. Who you choose to be to fulfill your purpose and your mission is your how. Later, you'll see that this is your secret sauce to standing out.

Our mission isn't something we discover. Rather, we create our mission by fully experiencing life, trying new things, going outside a comfort zone, and discovering what the world needs. When we do this, we find ways to make the world better (purpose), and create new products, services, and experiences to activate that purpose (mission).

When we do this to our absolute best, we become who we need to be and embody the leadership that others need to help us make it happen. This comprises our legacy and will be what others say about us when we're gone.

Contrary to society's popular belief, you weren't put here to be exclusively a professional soccer player, a doctor, an investment banker, or a famous YouTuber. Further, you weren't predestined to do that one thing and challenged to try to find it. You were put here for much more than that.

How ridiculously challenging and unfair would it be if you were meant to discover and do only one thing for your entire lifetime? Considering life has infinite possibilities, there has to be more to it.

You're likely already feeling stress, confusion, and uncertainty in your heart and mind from trying to discover your purpose in life and you may or may not agree with the four beliefs that mean so much in my own life. That's okay, but I would encourage you to go back and reread the four beliefs in the form of a question. See what happens when you add "What if" to the beginning of each sentence. You should feel that familiar stress and uncertainty being replaced by a feeling of excitement and possibility.

THE THREE-PILLAR PURPOSE MODEL

Another way to relieve that stress of finding your purpose involves not only asking what if, but also coming to the realization that we all have the same three reasons for being here. We are meant to rise, shine, and impact. This is the three-pillar purpose model I mentioned earlier.

Embracing and living by this model will give you the power of feeling motivated, goal-oriented, flexible, and free to chase whatever it is you are driven to do within any given moment of your life.

You were put on this planet to perform three purpose-related functions.

1. **Rise.** To be the real you at your absolute best with the talents and gifts you were naturally given and maximizing the unlimited potential you have. Rising means starting a new day again, being better than you were the day before, being bigger than any challenge you face, enhancing your skills and abilities, and taking a higher road each and every day. You rise above problems, are more positive than negative, and push into greater things than you did the day before. Some call it peak performance. When you do this, other people feel and experience you at your

best. More importantly, you feel energy, pride, and joy because you did your absolute best. Think back to a time when you did your best at something and remember how it felt. You felt that way because you fulfilled a part of your purpose. Imagine the feeling of being your best or getting better all the time!

2. **Shine.** To lead to help others rise, develop teams, collaborate across boundaries, innovate, inspire and lead change, create a new vision for your world and those around you, and do all the things that great leaders do. Shining means that you cast a light of possibility, vision, optimism, learning, development, and other qualities of great leadership on people, functions, organizations, and communities (no matter how small or how large). To be able to shine your leadership light onto others, you first need to lead yourself to be your best. Some people try to skip the first purpose pillar and when they do, we see them as managers.

3. **Impact.** To make a difference and leave the world a little better than you found it. Once you rise to your best self and lead others to be their best, together you can change the world and make life better for others. To have impact means your presence and place on Earth has meaning today, tomorrow, or over the course of your lifetime. That meaning could be as small as doing something for one stranger, or as big as impacting the world by creating a product, service, or experience that changes the lives of millions. Either way, you make a difference.

By approaching every day, every decision, and every goal with a mindset that incorporates those three pillars of purpose, you will transform the way you think, act, and feel. Your purpose becomes clear and you relieve so much of the stress that you have to find your singular purpose. You will feel the energy and excitement to challenge yourself to rise, shine, and impact every day and you open the door to endless possibilities to find a mission or missions to fulfill that purpose.

As we talked about in earlier chapters, a critical element to making this all happen starts with planning, being more intentional, and in control of your day. You exist to rise, shine, and impact and it doesn't just happen to you. You have to make it happen for you. Start each day (or prepare the night before) by asking yourself a few important questions.

- How will I get better today?
- How do I show my best self today?
- Who needs my leadership today?
- Can my leadership create, improve, or change an existing aspect in my current (personal or professional) role?
- How can I make a difference (small or large) today by touching the life of someone else?
- How can I make things a little better today than they were yesterday? Or is there a major cause or mission I can advance on today?
- What will I do to measure how I fulfilled my purpose today (best self, leadership, making a difference)?
- What feeling do I want at the end of the day because I lived my purpose and who will I share that feeling with?

Using the three-pillar purpose model for your life means you are exemplifying what it means to stand out in this world.

GROWTH WITHIN THE THREE PILLARS

Now that you're familiar with the three pillars of rise, shine, and impact, it's important to realize that each one has three steps embedded within them to make that pillar possible (again, the power of three).

The three steps are consistent for each and form three swim lanes that cut across all three pillars. These are (in order): learning, planning, and executing. All three swim lanes are unique and build on each other. The totality of the levels reveals a process for activating and tracking how well you're living the three-pillar purpose model.

These simple but powerful levels flow in a linear manner like the various color belts that signify rank and expertise in martial arts or the graduating grade levels in school. As you grow smarter, stronger, and better at each pillar, you are able to more effectively take the next step in your growth, development, and life purpose. Your best self leads to better leadership, and better leadership leads to more impact in the world.

To explain the swim lanes in a little more detail...

First, you learn more about the level in which you're in. It could be learning more about yourself to be the best you, learning how to be a leader, or learning about what the world needs so you know how to have an impact. With this new awareness and knowledge, you begin to think differently, and this allows you to act differently and with more purpose.

Next, you begin to set goals, make plans, and strategize how to accomplish those goals. You create specific steps for using this information and develop a vision for the future that leverages what you've learned. Many people do well in the first swim lane (learn). What starts to separate some people from the rest is the planning phase and having a specific set of goals, strategies, and tactics for doing what you want to do and being who you want to be. Planning and setting goals serve as the bridge between your thoughts and actions, which helps to determine your future.

Finally, you execute on those ideas, goals, and plans by consistently doing the necessary work. You embody what it's like to be your best self and be a leader. You set the example for others and you do what it takes to make an impact for others. This is how you stand out.

The key is to understand that everyone learns, few set real plans and goals, and even fewer put those actions into motion. Standouts go the extra step and stick with those actions more consistently and longer than others and therefore achieve better results. They're adaptable and able to adjust their goals, strategies, and tactics as necessary to achieve a desired outcome. The more they take action, the greater the probability of success and the more opportunities they have to stand out. This is the great separator.

It's also important to recognize that this model recognizes that you, your circumstances, and the world is constantly changing. You learn as you go and adjust plans based on your changing world, surroundings, feedback, and always-evolving thoughts and ideas. Therefore, it's also possible to reassess who you are, what you want, and where you're going at any given time.

Within this model, you're always free to go back to a certain level, depending on your situation, changes in life, or a new chosen destination. For example, if you make a life or career change, you may need to go back to the beginning and learn about yourself again. Then, build a new personal development plan and set new goals, act as your new self, and start to make a difference in a different way.

This model is clear and purposeful. Let's explore how these swim lanes manifest across all three pillars and create a nine-level growth, development, and results model that you can follow.

Rise

1. **Learn about yourself.** Learn as much as you can about who you really are. Think about what you like and don't like. Explore your strengths and weaknesses. Discover your core values. Find out what makes you tick and what energizes you. This is best achieved when you know yourself in the past, in the present, and in the future (who you want to be). The more you know about yourself, the easier and clearer everything else becomes.

2. **Set goals and build a personal development plan.** Develop short-term and long-term plans for being your best self now and becoming the person you want to be in the future. This would also involve your career, life goals, and aspirations. This is your destination that we talked about before. For maximum effectiveness, share those plans with others who will hold you accountable and help shape the results.

3. **Work the plan to be your best you.** Act in accordance

with the real you and your plans. Work consistently hard each day to become the person you want to be and do the things you want to do. Lead yourself by bringing out your best. Grow and develop your skills, talents, emotional intelligence, awareness, and knowledge and other attributes and qualities of your best self. This is what separates the standouts from the rest.

Shine

4. **Learn about leadership.** After you learn to lead yourself, you can begin to learn how to lead people, processes, changes, and functions. It takes time, knowledge, and awareness to learn what it means to be a great leader. The more you know about you and the more you know about leadership, the better leader you will be.

5. **Set leadership goals and a leadership development plan. Then, practice being a leader.** Develop a plan for who you want to be as a leader. Discover what an effective leader does for your company, community, family, or whatever you're involved with. Practice and develop your leadership style in smaller situations and one-on-ones with others. Similar to practicing a sport or developing your skills, you must have a strategy for leadership and practice it with due diligence. You aren't born a leader; you become a leader.

6. **Embody true leadership for others.** Put that leadership plan into action and exemplify your leadership greatness. Work each day to model your leadership best and shine your leadership light on others. Over time, you'll build trust, credibility, competence, and confidence because

you will be demonstrating your leadership by making a difference in your home, community, organization, and the world. However, you must work through levels one through five to fully activate this level.

Impact

7. **Learn about opportunities.** Learn as much as you can about your job, business, community, and the world. The more you know, the more you can do. Knowledge is power and your power is profit. Identify what needs to be fixed, changed, or created. What does your company, customer, and the world need? Anchor those opportunities for impact to the things you do best and have the most interest in doing.

8. **Develop a strategic plan.** Develop a strategy to affect change, innovate, and create valuable new products or services. The more knowledge and information you have and the more training and experiences you have, the better you will be at putting together a game plan for solving the problems or capitalizing on the opportunities that you identified.

9. **Implement the plan and measure the impact.** Implement the strategy you developed. This is another instance where the best of the best stands out. Most people learn about their business or their part of the world and think about ways to make a difference. Standouts, however, execute on these ideas. The more you do and the more people you solve problems for, the greater your impact will be on the world. However, you can only achieve this level if you are the best that you can be, you are an effec-

tive leader, and you do the things that are required to make a difference in your organization or the world.

GRADUATING THE LEVELS WITH HONORS

It should be clear that reaching a certain level in the three-pillar purpose model requires completion of the work in the prior level. Completion of each level should create an opportunity for you in the next level and a growing opportunity for your life's purpose.

You should also be humble and take pride in your current achievement level. If you're a standout level two and you meet a fellow standout level eight, that's okay. That person was once in your shoes. Part of how they make an impact is to give back and help you shift from level two to level three. Ask that person for help and reach out to the standout community as well. It's our mission to help each other.

Wear your standout level as a badge of honor. Celebrate your progress from one level to the next. Then, make sure you pay it forward for the group coming up behind you.

The effectiveness to which you complete each pillar and each sublevel will determine the meaning that you give to your life, the value that you give to the world, and ultimately the value that you get in return. The output of work you put into each pillar will determine if you graduate to the next level *with honors*.

For example, the better person you become, the more people you will positively impact. The better leader you become, the more future leaders you'll develop. The more problems you solve or innovative things you create, the more people you'll impact. The more you do, the more honors you'll receive.

Imagine what it would be like at the end of your life if you graduate summa cum laude in personal development, leadership, and impact. Now imagine what would happen if thousands or millions of standouts did the same. What would that world look like?

THE THREE-PILLAR PURPOSE MODEL LEVELS IN ACTION

Here are a few other specific examples of how the graduating levels of the Three-Pillar Purpose model works:

- If you're just starting your journey, you're a level one standout. Everyone starts there either knowingly or unknowingly.
- Once you move deep into your personal development journey and develop into the person you want to become, you'll become a level three standout.
- If you are making a huge difference in your relationships, family, and community because of the person you've become, you might be a level three plus standout (the plus indicating an achievement of honors).
- If you create, train, and develop ten other leaders, you would be a level six plus standout.
- If you have a significant impact on the world and create a service that improves the lives of thousands of people, you might proudly proclaim that you are a level nine plus standout. This isn't about how many followers you have on social media, it's about how many of your followers

are better off because of who you are, what you did and what you offer to inspire and help them.

As I said before, life itself has a lot of twists and turns. You can't control many of them, but you can control what you do as a result of them. You might need to leave a relationship and go back to level one to learn and become who you really are. At some point, you might need to make a career change and go back to level four to learn how to be a new leader with new skills in a new field. The model is powerful, flexible, and inspiring. It's a simple but highly effective way to track your journey.

THE THREE PILLARS ALREADY EXIST IN YOUR LIFE

The three-pillar purpose model is more powerful than you realize, mostly because it already exists in the natural world. Doesn't life itself follow the three pillars?

You spend your early years learning, growing, and developing your skills and knowledge. Hopefully, you're working to become the best version of the adult you can be.

Later, you move into a career, and (hopefully) assume the role of a leader, either directly by leading other people, functions, or businesses, or by being a leader in your field.

As you progress toward becoming a better you and assume a leadership role, you start to focus on ways you can make a difference. In your elderly years, you will look back and hope you made a difference. Ideally, you left a legacy and had a lasting positive impact on the world.

This three-pillar model is also what recruiters, companies, and others seek when hiring people to work for their company. They want to find, attract, and retain workers who are the very best at what they do, have the ability to be future leaders in the organization and will have a positive impact on the business or their team.

Most interviewees focus on their accomplishments, work experiences, and skills. Standouts, however, clearly articulate who they are, what they do, how they will step into a leadership role (with or without a title), and the impact they will have on the organization. They can clearly communicate a vision for the interviewer of the benefits of hiring them. The same mindset works for getting a promotion once you're in an organization.

Besides career achievement, the three pillars are what we ask of others in life and what others ask of us. After all, don't we want our children, significant others, teams, and everyone around us to bring their best and lead by assuming ownership of certain things? We also want them to do something with themselves that impacts other people.

Your purpose is the three pillars. As you write and live out the story of your life, you work to become your own hero, lead to guide others to be their best, and become a legend by making an impact on people and the world that outlives your time on Earth.

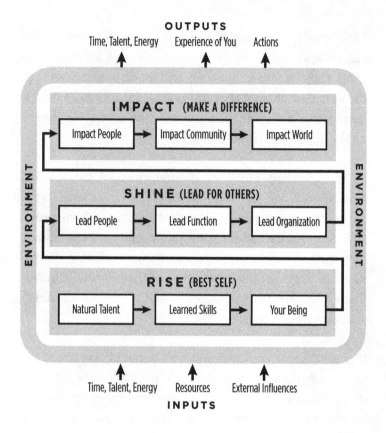

OUTPUTS
Time, Talent, Energy   Experience of You   Actions

IMPACT (MAKE A DIFFERENCE)

Impact People → Impact Community → Impact World

SHINE (LEAD FOR OTHERS)

Lead People → Lead Function → Lead Organization

RISE (BEST SELF)

Natural Talent → Learned Skills → Your Being

ENVIRONMENT

Time, Talent, Energy   Resources   External Influences
INPUTS

ACTIVATORS

The three-pillar purpose model itself is a very powerful tool for living a purposeful life. It's a new way of thinking and approaching your purpose that creates energy, inspiration, freedom, and direction. For maximum effectiveness, there are three powerful activators to the model you need to initiate.

Control Your Inputs

It's crucial to control your inputs to the model, because the outcomes will be directly affected by whatever you put into it.

The higher quality and quantity your inputs are, the higher the quality and quantity your outputs will be. This is similar to a top athlete or high-performance automobile. If you eat bad food, you will feel unhealthy. If you view negative stories or socialize with negative people, you will think negatively and become pessimistic.

Standouts are strict about what they take in so they can optimize what they put out. Controlling your inputs is all about using your available resources to generate the highest quality output, service, or experience of you. Remember that you get out of something what you put into it, including yourself.

You can't be your best self, your best leader, and make the greatest impact if your inputs are negative, unhealthy, and unproductive. After all, you can't build a great product with bad parts and processes.

Leverage Your Environment

To enhance each of the three pillars, you must optimize your environment. This means you have the right people, the right places, the right processes, and the right things around you. It means that your physical location maximizes your time and available resources. For some, this means being closer to work, near the right gym, living with or close to the right people, and being in areas that minimize wasted time.

The best entertainers, C-suite leaders, and other standouts have a top team around them including financial advisors, coaches, mentors, and publicists. They also have the right spaces around them to inspire creativity, innovation, and peak performance. You can enhance your purposeful environment by living in and around places that allow you to maximize standout endeavors and minimize wasted time and effort.

Your environment should match your core values and inspire and help you to succeed and be happy. If you live for the outdoors, be in outdoor places and live in a home with a lot of natural light and beautiful views. If you're energized by challenging activities, live in the city, and have more physical activity items around the house.

Use your environment as a reflection of who you are and to bring out your best. Your environment, including and most importantly your spouse or partner, will ultimately determine your success and happiness.

Control and Maximize Your Outputs

Third and most important, the learning, planning, and actions of standouts creates the outputs that have optimal impact on others and creates the most value. Standouts recognize that their outputs become someone else's inputs and those inputs create outputs in others, which perpetuates the cycle further. This is how one person can create a ripple effect on others. If you want to make a difference and give your life meaning, determine and control your outputs.

What you give is always what you get back.

If your output is filled with negativity and pessimism, what do you think you will attract around you?

If you're full of energy and joy, what do you think you will attract in return?

Your inputs become your thoughts, your thoughts become your beliefs, your beliefs become your actions, your actions become your habits, and your habits become your results. Your results then become the inputs and the value you get in return.

The value of your inputs is directly related to the value of your outputs and vice versa.

Output or Input?

Most people think of money as an output. They think if they work hard, get promoted, and get the fancy title, they'll make more.

More money means you can buy more, do more, and have more security in life. It's the means to an end.

Standouts, however, view money as an input. They see it as a valuable resource like time, energy, and talents. Standouts are more focused on how they can use their inputs and resources to feed back into the purpose pillars and drive outputs that impact others.

The more money standouts make, the more they can reinvest in themselves or into the product, service, or experience they offer. This allows them to do more for others. Standouts consider money to be the input that fuels and grows the never-ending circle of value for others.

This alternative view of money is why a standout's legacy is not about how much money they make, it's about the impact they have in the world.

THOUGHTS ON LEAVING A LEGACY

When you're much older (in your seventies or eighties), you're going to look back and wonder if you lived your best life, made a difference in the world, and accomplished all the goals and objectives you wanted to fulfill. You will think deeply about the person you became, who you helped, and how you impacted those closest to you and the larger community around you. More holistically speaking, you'll ponder how you will leave the world a better place.

Standouts start with the end in mind. Like a master chess player, they have a vision or an idea about how something should be, could be, or needs to be, and then they work backwards to figure out how to get there.

One last thing, the best career advice that I ever received was about following my vision and my mission. My mentor, good friend, and executive coach once advised me to never attach myself to a person, company, place, project, or status symbol like titles, money, or assets. He said to attach to your purpose and mission. That is how you keep your peace, power, and sense of self-worth, as well as meaning.

You'll never be unhappy or feel unsuccessful if you follow the real reason you're here, and you stay true to why you do what you do and have what you have.

I encourage you to consider this three-pillar purpose model

deeply and align your future North Star. Use it in your approach to every day and each situation. As you will see in the next chapter, the three-pillars purpose model drives each step you take in your journey towards happiness, success, and standing out.

STAIRS TO HELP YOU LIVE YOUR PURPOSE

Today:

- Define what the best version of yourself is. Who are you? What do you do? How do you do it? What does it feel like to be at your best, and how will you know you are doing your best (in multiple areas of your holistic success life)?
- How do you lead to help others? What is your leadership style? What leaders do you admire and what can you do to emulate them and embody what they stand for? How will you know that you are a successful leader?
- How do you want to make an impact on the world? Start with your home, your community, your workplace, and then beyond. How is the world better because you were in it?
- To fully live your purpose, evaluate every source of your inputs, optimize everything (and everyone) that helps you, and eliminate everything and everyone that doesn't. Take a look at your environment and determine how you can make the people, places, and things around you work *for* you, not *against* you. Finally, take a look at your outputs and how other people see and feel you. What are the results of who you are and what you do?

Every day:

- In your journal or somewhere else, plan how you will get better today. What will you read, what skill will you work on, how will you improve your health or your relationships or your financial situation? How will you evaluate that you got better? What are those key moments for your best to shine and where is it not as important to be your best (to save energy for the things that really matter)?
- As a leader, who needs your inspiration, help, or support today? How will you connect with your team, key partners, and business leaders? What can you do to move a project forward? Is your team focused on the work that's important and is that work connecting to the broader vision?
- What impact will you make today? Who can you inspire, help, or make happy today? What small or large thing can you do today to make the people, processes, or environment around you better? What step can you take towards a project that will have a bigger impact later?
- Evaluate your inputs, outputs, and environment today. What worked and what didn't? What can you eliminate? What can you double down on? What can you add to your day to improve your inputs? How can you leverage your environment today?

Main goal: Define your purpose and live it every day.

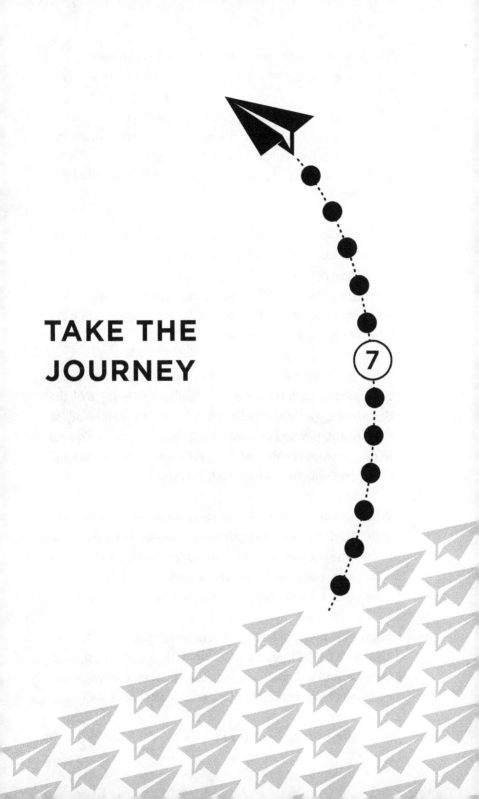

TAKE THE
JOURNEY

7

"The journey of a thousand miles begins with one step."

~LAO TZU (ANCIENT CHINESE PHILOSOPHER AND WRITER)

The late great Yogi Berra once said, "When you come to a fork in the road, take it." Believe it or not, there is profound wisdom in those words. After all, you can't be in two places at once, so you need to make a choice in the direction you want to take.

Without a doubt the worst thing you can do is to make no decision, stand still, and let life pass you by. You never get anywhere that way. At least, I think that's what Yogi was getting at. Maybe Will Rogers echoed this sentiment best when he said, "Even if you're on the right track, you'll get run over if you just sit there."

What you may not realize is that life is full of forks in the road. Going back to one of the guiding principles of the Standout Experience and a critical rule in the game of life, you are 100 percent in control of these decisions. You get to decide what you do and don't do, even if unexpected and uncontrollable things happen (and they will).

With each decision you make, you choose the path you take, which leads to another opportunity and another decision to make. The stacking effect of each of these decisions drives your days, weeks, months, years, and ultimately your life. That's why each day is your life in miniature.

Standouts make better decisions every day, regardless of how they feel. They choose to do what's difficult, uncomfortable, and unknown because they understand that these decisions have a compounding effect. The more good decisions you make, the greater the probability for success and happiness you'll achieve and the more opportunities you'll have to take new paths.

THE THREE CHOICES

Each morning when you wake up, you're faced with multiple decisions about what to wear, what to eat, which route to take to work, etc. Various sources point to a generally believed notion that we make about 35,000 choices per day, which is roughly 2,000 decisions per hour or one every two seconds.

The compounding effect of each decision leads to another decision that could be made on how you feel, what you're doing, where you are, what's happening around you, etc. Your decisions drive your days and determine your life.

In the past, your parents made these decisions for you and did the best they could to set you up for success. Now it's up to you. Every time life presents you with a fork in the road (a decision), you're in control to make one of three general choices (each with varying degrees of impact), thus again employing the power of three in your life.

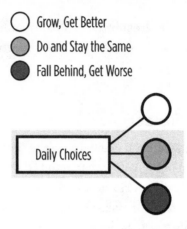

1. **Rise higher.** This is when you make the decision to rise, grow, improve, do more than you could before, exceed expectations and shift into new altitudes that you haven't experienced before. You make the conscious decision to learn new things, gain experience, enhance your skills, rise above challenges, and move towards your potential. This upward movement leads you in a positive direction to enhance the number of opportunities you'll receive or further your goals and objectives. Generally, it requires moving into the unknown above your comfort zone. This is always the harder choice to make and it requires strength, resilience, and often times doing what seems counterintuitive. By always rising, climbing upwards and going higher, you face the gravity of life and that's why it's hard. However, standouts push themselves to climb more consistently over a longer period of time. They raise the bar for themselves and over time, separate from the masses that are stuck on cruise control or worse.

2. **Stay the same.** This is the comfort zone in which most people live. To cruise through life is to consistently take the easier path, where more often than not, things

stay the same. There are some attempts to rise above the average, but an upward movement is usually offset (in the long run) by a downward fall (quite often a self-sabotage). Nothing destructive happens, but you don't gain any ground toward your goals and objectives. In a weird way, this is the worst possible outcome, because you learn nothing from the experience. At least if you pick a direction and fail, you'll acquire valuable knowledge about what not to do in the future. By choosing nothing, you also don't enhance anything in your career or your life. Many people work in this zone. Instead of challenging themselves with new opportunities, they stay in the same situation or the same job. They think they have five years of experience, but they actually have one year of experience relived five times. If you cruise and stay in the comfort zone for too long, you will lose ground to those who choose to rise higher.

3. **Fall behind.** Repeatedly making the wrong decisions takes you in the opposite direction of where you want to go. This is a slow and steady path to falling behind. Remember that many choices lead to short-term pleasure and that leads to long-term pain and vice versa. For example, eating too much unhealthy food can lead to many chronic health conditions, Alternatively, enduring the short-term pain of exercise can lead to long-term benefit in a fitter, stronger, and healthier body. The point is that you are going to experience pain one way or the other, so why not choose the short-term pain that creates long-term gains, instead of the short-term gains that lead to long-term pains. The lesson to be learned is to do what's hard now so you can live better later. Also remember that the cumulative effect of making bad deci-

sions creates a widening gap between where you are and where you want to be or where others are. The greater the gap, the more you feel unhappy and unsuccessful. Compounded bad decisions lead to an unhealthy body, a negative mindset, an uninspired heart, less opportunities, and worst-case scenarios while others are taking a different higher road or at worst, staying the same. Either way, you're creating a gap that makes it hard to recover from. At all costs, avoid the compounding decisions that could lead you to crash (drugs, alcohol, or other poor health choices, bad relationships, wrong jobs, and substandard environments).

The key to making one of these three choices is to take control and act intentionally. Think "if...then..." all the time. If you want to get healthier, then rise higher by choosing to... If you want to have a better relationship, then rise higher by choosing to...If you want to get that job or promotion, then rise higher by choosing to...

The effect of making the same type of decision (up, down, or the same) has a compounding effect that you don't see early, which is why so many people give up. But you will realize this in exponential impacts later (where the standouts play). Every 1 percent increase in each area of your life done every day will compound and further increase the slope of your exponential rise. This is called the aggregation of marginal gains.

AGGREGATION OF MARGINAL GAINS

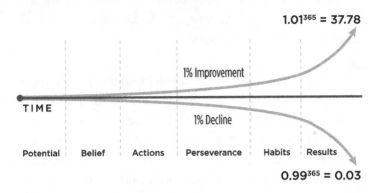

$$1.01^{365} = 37.78$$

1% Improvement

TIME

1% Decline

Potential　Belief　Actions　Perseverance　Habits　Results

$$0.99^{365} = 0.03$$

One of my favorite mentors, Darren Hardy, wrote a book explaining this phenomenon called *The Compound Effect.* In his book, he asks if you would rather have three million dollars right now or a penny that doubles in value every day for thirty-one days.

Most people would take the three million dollars and the easy, short-term success. At the end of thirty-one days, those people would still have the three million dollars, assuming it's not spent by then. Standouts, however, understand the wisdom in playing the long game. They have patience, do the hard work, and build for the bigger reward later.

Meanwhile, that penny, doubling every day for thirty-one days becomes $5.4 million!

One penny becomes two, and $2.50 becomes $5.00. Eventually, forty thousand becomes eighty thousand, which becomes one-hundred and sixty thousand, etc.

Whether you rise higher, stay the same, or fall behind, each choice leads to a new set of outcomes. While most people focus on the short term, immediate wins, losses, wants, and needs when making decisions, standouts play the long game and think many moves ahead.

Like a professional athlete, high-stakes poker player, chess champion, or any other top competitor in any game, standouts use the current move to set up the more important plays later in the game. They use the stacking effect to build one play on top of another, one decision on top of another, and one success on top of another. This builds momentum and elevates them to higher levels.

In terms of the Three-Purpose Pillar model, this is how you, as a standout, will elevate from your best self, to leadership, to higher impacts, and eventually to your legacy.

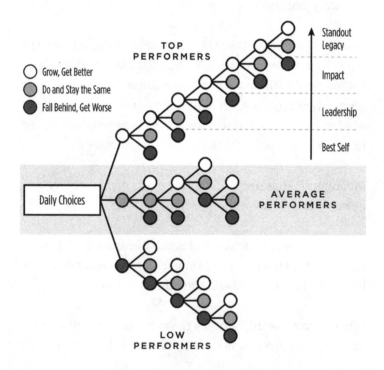

Standouts also enjoy the challenge of making choices and the game of life itself. They love the relentless chase upwards for success, happiness, and greatness. Standouts are dedicated to the process to get to their destination.

Starting the upward journey, however, is hard. It takes a lot of force to get going, but it gets easier once you build momentum. In this way, you are a lot like an airplane or rocket ship. It's hard to get off the ground and it takes a lot of effort to fight the forces of gravity. Once you reach cruising altitude or the earth's orbit, it becomes easier and momentum is on your side. It takes as much fuel for a rocket to launch as it does to orbit the earth many times.

In your own life, you are either climbing to new altitudes, cruising along at a steady altitude (while others may be rising higher than you), or you are in a downward spiral that eventually leads to you crashing. Always set the dial for the next altitude and use your own motivational fuel to propel you to that next level. The higher you go, the better the view.

THE END GAME

The choices you make will eventually lead to additional opportunities and ultimately your final destination. At the end of your life, you will look back and score yourself on who you became and what you did.

As you take this journey day-by-day, step-by-step, and decision-by-decision, you will keep that score based on how you react to the world around you or by the proactive approach you take to control your destiny. As you read earlier, it's important to know where you are heading and have GPS to help you get there.

Not only will having a destination in mind help you make better choices and feel more in control of your direction, but you will enjoy the satisfaction and happiness that comes from clarity. Generally, there are four types of destinations and four types of people who approach their journey in different ways.

1. **The Needle in the Haystack.** A small percentage of people know exactly what they want to do and who they want to be. They have a specific pinpoint in mind for what they want to do and when they want to do it. They're willing to do whatever it takes to get there, and we admire them for this focus, clarity, courage, and dedication. The downside is that they usually lack vision after they reach that one moment in time or that pinnacle in life. Once they start a new company and it becomes a stable-state entity, then what? Once they become an Olympic swimmer—for example—and retire, then what? Once they get to a company that they want to work for and at a level that they want to achieve, then what? The mind, body, heart, and soul are always looking for growth and new things. That's why the grass always looks greener somewhere else. The needle in the haystack seems wonderful and we want to be like those people, but do we really want that one and only one thing?

2. **The Mistaken Identity.** A moderately higher percentage of people have some vague notion of what they want to do, have, and achieve. However, their vision is not specific, focused, or holistic enough, and it's generally influenced

by external factors (society, peers, and parents). These people work hard to move toward something, but once they get there, they realize that the outcome is not their version of success and they aren't happy. They spend years doing and chasing the wrong thing only to realize it's too late and face the regret of those decisions.

3. **The Wanderers.** Most people don't know what they want or who they want to be. They wander aimlessly, follow their feelings and short-term desires, have as many ups as downs, leave their destiny to chance, and make reactionary decisions based on outside influences. Eventually, they look back and wonder "what if," and have more regrets than satisfaction. They feel like they have wasted their time and could have been in a better place if they could do it all over again. It's hard for this group to focus on the things they have, the experiences they've lived, and the people around them. Instead, they focus on the things they could have done, and they regret how much time they spent, in hindsight, not actually doing anything at all. They spent too much time waiting for that one thing to come to them or for someone to guide them, help them, or give them something. They moved aimlessly through time and space, and ended up exactly where they were going—nowhere.

4. **The Standouts.** The last group is most reflective of the Standout Experience. These people have the clarity to know what they want to do and who they want to be, but not to a myopic level of detail. In other words, they have the freedom and flexibility to make choices and operate within a cone of probability that is aligned with their original vision. In effect, they know what they want

to do and the impact they want to have, but they give themselves the flexibility and freedom on how to make it happen. They move to their North Star, but they're happy with degrees of variability as long as it's within the same general area.

For example, someone in this group might know they want to work with underprivileged kids in the southwestern area of the US (to be near family). This standout might, however, change from being a teacher in Los Angeles, to running an after-school camp in Arizona, to writing childrens' books in Las Vegas. In that scenario, their vision stays the same, but their what and how remains flexible to change. They enjoy different opportunities, but they also get immense satisfaction by always staying within a range of their core values and their why. It's a delicate balance between knowing exactly *what* but being flexible about the *how* and *where*. That's what makes it hard, but that's also why it's a Standout Experience.

If you fall into the category of the first group, great! If not, that's okay because you're not supposed to have it all figured out yet. After all, that's why you're reading this. The goal, of course, is to become that fourth group, who have the same clarity as the first personality type, but to also have the freedom and flexibility to stay within the goal in different ways.

To get there, it starts with the first few chapters of the book where you discover who you are and what your future is. It's having an attitude and way of thinking that life is a fun game worth playing and that you approach each day with love and happiness. You also spend each day focusing on your three-pillar purpose. With all of that as your being, way of thinking, and approach to life, you can more easily work towards a general idea of the lifestyle that you want and the person you want to be. Use these guiding principles to gain better clarity and to help you consistently move in a direction toward your potential, endless possibilities, and ultimately, your legacy.

TRAVELING ALONG THE DECISION TREE

Think of all the choices you make throughout your life as being individual branches on a decision tree. Take a few moments to reflect on the associated diagram that shows how the higher you climb along the tree, the more you develop your qualities of self, leadership, and impact. This is how you rise above all the variables trying to pull you down that will inevitably occur from time to time. As you examine the diagram, consider a few guiding principles to reaching a successful and happy life.

- Always choose the upward path toward what you want to do with your life, what the world needs from you, and for what you can get paid to do. By doing what others (parents, peers, career services) tell you to do, you'll traverse a different path that could lead to dissatisfaction and unhappiness. That path is like taking the blue pill in *The Matrix*, where you choose to play it safe and follow society's limitations for how you should live. This path will inevitably lead you to wonder what happened to your life and how to find purpose within it. Choosing the upward direction, however, is like taking the red pill, where you blaze your own trail. This path is always more difficult, but it always leads to a higher, happier, and more impactful destination. This is a much more rewarding journey, full of possibilities to achieve all your hopes and dreams.

- Strive for better, proactive decisions throughout the day that support your goals and dreams. Do what's hard and uncomfortable to grow and get better every day. Also, don't allow others to influence the decisions you make. It's your life, so you must make your own choices proactively and with clear intention.

- Raise the bar so that your standards keep rising higher. The mind, body, heart, and soul love to stretch and grow. This is known as resetting your average. You always have the potential to do more than you think you can. In Jesse Itzler's book, *Living with a SEAL*, he mentions how he learned that when people think they can't possibly run for another second, they're actually capable of running 40 percent longer. What this means for our purposes is that even when your instinct tells you you're exhausted and can't possibly go any further, you can actually go higher.

- Stop trying to avoid losses and go for wins. Be different and chase the possibilities of the higher unknown. Standouts are willing to take risks and within reason, absorb some losses to achieve what's possible. Like any good sports team or individual player, if you play it safe, you'll lose. If you're in control and play aggressively, you'll win.

- You can always chase the upside, but you must simultaneously protect the downside. While striving for what's possible (or what may seem impossible), be smart enough to have a safety net that catches you if you fall from the tree. Play the "and" game by being smart, having a game plan, and getting help when you need it. You can work hard to be a professional athlete but get an education to fall back on. You can also follow your passion to be a photographer but make money, save, and invest so you can afford your lifestyle and have wealth when you're done. Have the courage to go after that person you always wanted to date but be comfortable in who you are so it's okay if it doesn't work out. Walk your version of the high-wire act, but make sure you construct a safety net in case you fall. You might even be able to use that net to bounce more quickly back up.

- If you don't know the exact direction to reach your success and happiness, make decisions and climb the branches that carry you in an upward trajectory anyway. The point is that you are always moving forward and upward to something. Sometimes, you might need to jump to another branch to create more opportunities and be able to climb higher than you would if you stayed on the same branch. This might mean moving to a new industry, learning a new skill, or changing your job. This is also the most proactive way to be in control of your career, rather than waiting for someone else to decide your fate. My greatest opportunities and successes have come from leaving the possibilities on the branch I was currently traveling to take a risk of something greater on a different branch.

- Do what's hard now to create a better life for yourself in the future. More opportunities will surface that way as well. Anything great and worth having comes at a price with its own difficulties and challenges. Things don't just come to you. Avoid taking the easy path and doing what everyone else is doing now, because that will make your life harder in the future. Choose the more difficult path and always challenge yourself to push harder. Do more than you think you can, conquer your fears, move out of your comfort zone, and stretch yourself. That increasingly more difficult incline will lead you to higher places and bigger and better things.

BE MINDFUL OF OUTSIDE INFLUENCES

This is a key topic worth its own section. Always be in control of your path and push yourself in the direction you want to go. Don't be pulled by others or influenced to take a path that doesn't align with what you have learned about yourself or your future. This leads down a path that they want you to take, generally for their own purposes, and takes you farther away from the life's branch that you want to be on or should be on.

For the rest of your life, other people's decision trees will cross paths with yours. Some will come from below and carry you up. Others will come from above and drag you down. As we said before, inputs are critical and so is your environment. Ensuring you have the right outside influences is key to taking the upward path to your success.

Recognize that inputs can be ideas, situations, experiences, and other people. Remember that a very critical element of you as a Standout Experience is that your outputs are another person's inputs. The Standout Experience is all about the positive experience of you. Are you the person that lifts others to rise up, or are you a negative influencer that drags others down? Or do you stay in the zone of average as just another face with the rest of the crowd?

As you move through life, other people and therefore other decision trees will intersect with yours. They will come in and out of your life. If the moment is right, this can provide an outstanding opportunity to join forces and create even more impact.

It's also important to understand which of these "crossed

paths" is short term, medium term, or more long term. Many times, being unhappy and unsuccessful comes from treating a short-term crossed path like it's a long-term play for you. Know who and what to keep for the long journey, who and what to get rid of (and when), and who and what to keep for a certain period of time.

Don't stay in a job that is only meant for you to acquire a certain skill or build a certain network.

Don't stay in a relationship that only gives you a narrow and unhealthy experience of that person.

Don't keep working on a major when you only need to take a few classes to get the relevant knowledge you need.

Making this distinction in your life more consistently and better than others will help determine if you will stand out later.

Be mindful, however, when paths cross. It's your responsibility to make educated decisions about whether outside influences are good or bad. It can also be helpful to know which provide temporary/short-term help and which provide longer—perhaps permanent—benefits.

Harvard social psychologist, Dr. David McClelland, found that you are the average of the five people you spend the most time with. More specifically, he stated that the people with whom you mostly associate determine as much as 95 percent of the successes or failures you have in life.

McClelland's research reinforces the importance of interacting with positive people and keeping the right people in your life for either the short term or the long term. You're in control of who and what you want to be around.

BE AWARE OF THE GAPS

As you read earlier in this chapter, unhappiness and feeling unsuccessful is when growing gaps exist between where you are and where you want to be.

Relationships fail because two people travel different paths and gaps widen (they grow apart). This is the classic case of how two people can grow apart even though they appeared to be so well matched at one point in their lives. The gap between the paths of their lives gets too wide.

Job dissatisfaction occurs most often when your goals and objectives aren't properly matched to the work you're doing or the company that employs you. A gap can break open if a difference exists between your boss's expectations and what you deliver. Ultimately if that gap gets too wide, you could lose your job or get stuck in the same role with no hope for advancement.

The more you stay the same or travel on a downward path, the wider the gap becomes of job dissatisfaction. This will also create an internal gap where you fail to meet your own expectations, which can lead to unhappiness, regret, and other negative emotions.

New opportunities and happiness on the job occur when you're growing, enhancing your skills, and staying aligned with other people's expectations of your performance and abilities. When you reach a branch higher than the job itself can provide, that's when you get promoted and achieve higher levels of success.

Remember, you determine which relationships to be a part of and which jobs you want to perform. Don't hesitate if you see a gap forming in either one, because the longer you let it continue, the harder it will be to jump off that decision tree branch and start climbing a new one. Therefore, as soon as you spot the widening of a gap or feel complacency settling into a relationship, job, or other aspect of your journey, pivot and start something new and exciting.

Don't play in the safe zone and expect that someone will hand you a higher branch of the tree. You have to climb there yourself!

MOVING FORWARD

You've now completed another step of the playbook on your way to The Standout Experience, and you have worked through the second part of your basic human need. This is an exciting time because you've been exposed to new ideas and you've started to take actions to achieve more "clarity" about who you are and where you're going. You've also achieved more "simplicity" by reframing how you think and what you know to make better decisions and achieve higher levels of performance.

In the third and final section, you will learn how to create more "certainty" by doing things that separate you from the crowd and increasing your opportunities, your possibilities, and your probability of success and happiness.

The next chapter will discuss how to build the necessary foundations you need in your standout journey. After all, any relationship, career, life, or even physical structure is only as good as its foundation.

In the penultimate chapter of this next section, you'll learn how all of these steps in the playbook lead to how you can and will stand out when it matters most.

The final chapter will close your journey with an inspirational message and visual metaphor to radiate your standout experience on others for the rest of your life and beyond.

STAIRS TO HELP YOU TAKE THE JOURNEY

Today:

- With an end destination in mind, connect where you are now (Point A) with your goals later (Point B) through micro steps daily and weekly.
- What key events, opportunities, or defining moments are coming up in the next week, month, or quarter and what can you do to prepare for them now?
- What SOP (standard operating procedure) do you have in place for when something unexpectedly wrong happens? How will you respond and keep moving forward?
- How will you decide what to do or not do? Are you clear on your core values and guiding principles? Who will you go to for guidance?
- How will you take the higher road, improve, and get better every day? What risks and experiments are you willing to take?

Every day:

- Across all your most important success factors today, did you improve, stay the same, or decline? Rate yourself a 3.0 or a 2.0 or a 1.0 and add up your scores. Is your score higher than the previous day? Are you consistently above the average (2.0)?
- What difficult choices did you have to make today and were they good or bad? How can you do better tomorrow? What would your past self have done? Did your newer standout self compete and win against your old self?
- What risks did you take today? What new things did you do or take in to help you grow? What failures did you learn from? What outside influences did you experience today and how did you take the higher road and rise above them?
- What are the key steps you need to take tomorrow to continue to climb?

Main goal: Know the journey you're about to go on, take the right step each day, and enjoy the process.

PART 3

CERTAINTY

"People prefer the certainty of misery to the misery of uncertainty."

~VIRGINIA SATIR

BUILD YOUR
FOUNDATIONS

8

"The loftier the building, the deeper must the foundation be laid."

~THOMAS KEMPIS

Everything in life is created on foundations that were built earlier. Similarly, your standout journey is ultimately determined by what you learn and do today.

To build your foundation you must lay one brick at a time and do it consistently each day through trial and error and repeated behaviors. As Will Smith once said, "You don't set out to build a wall. You lay each brick as perfectly as a brick can be laid. You do that every day and soon you have a wall."

After your foundation is built, you will need to strengthen that structure on a daily basis. The last thing you want is for your foundation to crack and eventually crumble, because its durability will enable you to build one success after another on top of it.

The people who stand out at work, during games or competitions, and in life focus more on preparing in private than performing in public. They know it's what they do in practice that determines how well they play in the game. As the Navy SEALs' saying goes, "Under pressure, you don't rise to the occasion, you sink to the level of your training."

In other words, no one watches when the wall is being built, but everyone admires the wall once it's done.

In *The Seven Habits of Highly Effective People*, Stephen Covey explains that if you want to saw down a tree, you don't work harder and longer on the tree itself. Instead, you spend time sharpening the saw first, which enables you to be more productive with a stronger blade.

NBA All-Star Damian Lillard said, "If you want to look good in front of thousands, you have to outwork thousands in front of nobody."

The great soccer star Lionel Messi said, "It took me 17 years and 114 days to become an overnight success."

The importance of preparing backstage before you can stand out onstage can't be overstated. The actions you take every day with the information and knowledge you have will determine how far you go. The great differentiator is what you do different, better, and more often than the rest. Standouts aren't born; they're created.

The good news is you don't have to prepare alone in private. You already know to surround yourself with the right people. Look to coaches, trainers, leaders, and others you trust to provide great guidance and help you prepare, but make sure they're the right people in your development circle by asking these key questions:

- Does this person truly know me and understand my situation and future desires?
- What is their real motivation and are they acting in my best interest? (Are they actually invested in *me* or *their role*?)
- Have they done it before, and would I trade places with them? (Do their actions back up their words?)
- Have others vouched for their ability to provide guidance? (Do others back up their words?)

- Can they help me achieve a goal or next step?
- Is this person considered an expert in their field or a chosen topic?

These questions will help you determine how much value you place on the inputs you receive from others toward building your own walls and working hard in private. Keep in mind what you read earlier—whatever you see, hear, or take in, be sure to make it your own and that it fits in your personal playbook. Take what you get from others. Customize those inputs and personalize them to fit who you are, where you're going, and how you want to get there.

THINK STRATEGICALLY, NOT TACTICALLY

There are tactical things to do like choose a school and a major, graduate, get a job, and start to build your life. Take plenty of time to think about these decisions to make the choice that is right for you and your destination.

Ultimately, these seemingly important and difficult choices won't matter as much as you (or others) think in the long run. There are too many examples of wildly successful people who never went to college, didn't go to an Ivy League school, didn't get the best grades, started in a different career, or spent years not knowing what to do.

Standouts understand that the goals of these early years are broader than the tactical decisions they need to make. They recognize that the strategic foundations they build today will determine their future success, happiness, and unique abilities to standout no matter what job, industry, or in what life situation they're performing. They know that their foundation is flexible and remains relevant no matter what changes take place. If they place one brick in their wall and it doesn't quite fit, they replace the brick with another one before the mortar dries and other bricks rest on that foundation.

THE 10-10-10 FOUNDATIONAL PRINCIPLES MODEL

While most people get degrees, work on skills to get promoted, and meet people to help them achieve a specific task (e.g., get a job), standouts focus on the broader building blocks that support their long-term success in school, work, and life. These foundational principles increase the number of opportunities they get, improve their probability for success, provide for better decision-making, leverage the compound benefits of each decision, and accelerate their growth and development through the nine-level purpose model discussed earlier.

These core and standout building blocks serve as your foundation for success in school, on the job, and in life. What matters less is what the actual building blocks are. What matters more is that you have a strategy that works for you and you lay your own building blocks to support you now and what you will be in the future.

I have my own building blocks that I call the 10-10-10 Foundational Principles model. I share this with you not as a "do exactly this" task, but as a guide for what you could do or as ideas that might generate your own 10-10-10 principles. The key is that you have them and you work on them in private so that you will stand out in public when it matters most.

The most essential building blocks and the first ten foundational principles support a happy, healthy, and successful life. Without these, you might run the risk of negatively impacting some other part of your life. For example, having money problems or being unhealthy could make a difference in your job performance. Leveraging these foundational principles is essential to avoiding such a negative input from influencing your life.

1. **Create a budget and develop a long-term financial strategy.** Learn how to save and spend wisely. Those who make more deposits than withdrawals create the greatest value and a safety net in case something goes wrong. The more you save and invest, the more flexibility you'll have to do what you want, when you want, and with who you want in the future.

2. **Develop a health and fitness plan.** See a doctor regularly and set fitness goals for one year, three years, five years, and ten years later. That way, you'll know what success in this area will look like later in life. If you have a healthy body, it's much easier to have a healthy mind, heart, and soul. This leads to a healthier quality of life. Also, the more energy you have, the better you'll perform in many other areas of life.

3. **Create a lifelong learning plan.** Make a list of the books you want to read and the podcasts to which you want to listen. Identify conferences or workshops you'd like to attend. Schedule a proper amount of time for learning every day. Extend the idea of continuous learning to create a long-term holistic plan for success. Go to school

every day, and test and adjust the path accordingly. Also, get help along the way. The more you know, the more you grow, and the more you show. Leaders are readers, and the most successful people never stop learning.

4. **Set up your ideal environment.** Think about how far you're willing to travel to get to work. From there, decide on where you should live and the companies at which you'll seek employment. Resolve to spend most of your time with the people who make you better and happier. Set up any additional variables that allow you to achieve your goals and objectives like where you live, what and who is consistently around you, and what you read, watch, listen to, and take in. The better your environment, the better you will be. We are a product of our environment.

5. **Establish and practice your daily routine.** Have a preset schedule for fitness, learning, planning, reflection, downtime, fun, working on key projects, etc. This is such an important principle that there is an entire section dedicated to it later in this chapter. You now know that your daily growth and upward movement determines what you will be able to rise and aspire to. Your happiness and success will be determined by your daily routine.

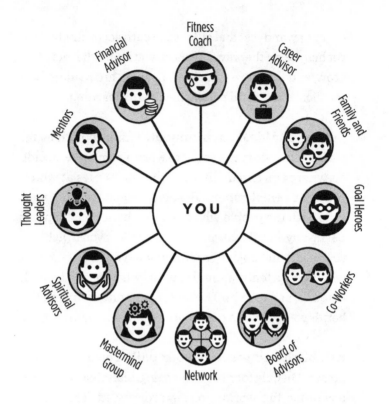

6. **Build your team.** Identify the coaches, mentors, professionals, experts, and peers you can go to for guidance, help, and answers. This includes your most intimate relationship. Your happiness and success are directly related to the people you spend the most time with. Have a personal board of directors that you check in with and report on your progress while seeking strategic guidance on how to move forward. Have a short-term mastermind group that helps you get through a particular class, problem, or project.

7. **Experiment and take risks but have a safety net.** Much of the success of your journey is determined by the risks you take, the experiments you attempt, and the failures

from which you learn. These actions clarify your mission and end goals by helping you to determine what you enjoy most and how you can help the world. Don't be afraid to try something new, but always have a safety net (e.g., minimum amount of money you need in the bank) and plan an exit strategy when possible.

8. **Gain real-world experiences.** Participate in activities that enhance your goals and definition of success. Travel to new places, try new jobs, build your strengths, expose yourself to new ideas and concepts. The more you learn from these things, the more you grow personally and professionally. You will also be exposed to things that you might not know that you like or don't like until you get exposed to them. More importantly, the more robust your experiences are, the more fulfilling your life will be.

9. **Learn what you enjoy in life and know how to deal with adversity.** Recognize what makes you happy, how you release stress, and where you do your best thinking. Plan appropriately and know what to do and who you can turn to for help when things go wrong.

10. **Create your bucket list.** Even if you're still young, create a list of all the things you want to do in your life. Don't wait until it's too late to enjoy some of the crazy and not-so-crazy things you want to accomplish or experience. A bucket list is one of the most inspirational and motivational things that you can do for yourself.

WHAT TO DO IN SCHOOL

So much negativity exists around getting a college degree

these days. Student loans, antiquated teaching methods, standardized exams, and the overwhelming student pressure has created massive dysfunction.

I believe the opposite. Post-high school education remains a fabulous option, and there is a lot of value that can be gained from colleges, universities, trade schools, and other learning and development opportunities during this time.

Tremendous resources and opportunities await you, regardless of the path you choose. There are many foundational things you can do to prepare for the world beyond your education and training. Some of these are basic tactics, but others are broader in terms of how to think and execute once you leave the safe harbor of the school system.

1. **Pick a field of interest based on your self-awareness and personal *ikigai*.** Pursue the things you would choose to learn and develop even if you didn't get paid to do them or have a grade attached to them. When selecting your major, minor, electives, and extracurricular activities, think about what you're great at, what ignites your internal fire, what will provide the most opportunities, and what can be leveraged across multiple industries or jobs.

2. **Develop two or three key skills that complement each other.** This is the time to experiment with different skills to discover the ones you're naturally best at and enjoy doing the most. This is ultimately what you want to be known (and hired) for. You'll need to not only combine skills to produce an additive effect to the value of your personal brand, but being adaptive enough to consistently reinvent yourself when necessary will be

essential to remaining relevant in the minds of tomorrow's employers. Your ability to quickly pivot, learn a new skill, and master it will be critical to highlighting the impact of which you're capable and position you ideally for sustained success. The more you can stack complementary skills and be great at those interdependent skills, the greater your chances of standing out.

3. **Use all your career services resources.** This one is the easiest but least utilized resources. Many students never visit career services. Others take advantage of only a small sample of its offerings. Look deeply into what career services can do for you and maximize that value. Like many other resources, you will get whatever you put into it.

4. **Leverage other resources that you can only get while in school (student discounts and connections).** You will likely never have this opportunity again, so absorb as much of it as you can while you can. Before you know it, everything will come at full cost and you will find less time to use all these resources. The more resources at your disposal, the more things you will be able to create and build.

5. **Understand how you learn and retain the information.** Know how and when to apply your lessons learned for success. Understanding how you learn, how you remember things best, and how you apply what you learn will enable you to repeat your successes. This valuable realization will be immensely helpful later in your professional life.

6. **Continue to learn about yourself (likes, dislikes) and**

experience new things. Knowing what you don't like is equally as important as knowing what you do like. Success and happiness come from addition *and* subtraction.

7. **Try, fail, and experiment with life's foundational elements while in school.** College is the ideal place to do this, because it's an opportunity to learn just as much about life as your chosen craft or career aspirations. This is the time to experiment, take risks, and be more courageous when you have less on the line and less to lose, with everything to gain. That represents opportunity within opportunity!

8. **Build a wide and deep network of mentors, advisors, and standouts while in school and after graduation.** This network can prove a powerful alliance in your standout journey. Know which people are your deep, ongoing, and consistent connections and which are the shorter, potentially *one-time,* long-tail connections. You'll need both. Studies have shown that many of your best connections will be the ones you don't know well but are willing to connect you with someone they know who can help you.

9. **Gain experiences relevant to your interests, required skills, and industry.** This background will help you to determine what you want to do for work and in your life. This will also allow you to build your foundations for later. You can practice your skills, work on your craft, learn from others around you, and apply what you learned in one place to another.

10. **Create and/or join a community of standouts who**

work together and support the concepts in this book.
Keep this book handy and refer to it as often as needed, especially when anticipating a standout moment or opportunity to have a positive impact. Find others who are in the Standout Movement and work with each other to take the journey. Compete against each other, help each other, share what you learn and do. Part of the three pillars of purpose is to be your best, but remember that it's also to lead others to be their best.

WHAT TO DO AT WORK

One of the most important things you can do to set yourself up for a successful career is to have a plan for your first thirty, sixty, and ninety days on the job, and manage the many transitions you'll face in your career. The more effectively you plan for taking on a new job, moving to a new industry, or having more responsibility, the more successful you'll be at work.

There are a number of books on this topic and I recommend you read one of them. My ten foundational principles are slightly different, but they worked for me to quickly rise from an intern to an executive at Disney. They can also be leveraged to help you understand what you need to do in your first or second job. When executed diligently, they should also help to set you up for the highest probability of success.

1. **Pick the right job.** First and foremost, you need to choose the right job for the right reason. Just like the personal and lifestyle reasons that I chose Disney after graduation, you must choose the right job. Your happiness depends

on it. Most people choose a job and then attempt to fit a life around it. Standouts define the lifestyle they want and fit their job around that. They maintain balance and integrate their personal life with their professional life. Standouts know that a personal life has the potential to impact job performance and vice versa. Figure out how you can achieve a healthy balance of both by experimenting with ways you can bring them together, but always prioritize your life first. You are the most important thing in your life.

2. **Learn the expectations and your areas of responsibility for the role.** Learn how and what it means to exceed expectations. Standouts do what others avoid and they know what is expected of them and how to go beyond what is expected. If you only do what everyone else does, you will not be able to stand out. Practice executing your key technical skills, maintaining positive energy, people skills, and leadership efforts.

3. **Set annual goals and create a plan with your team leader or boss about how you will achieve those goals.** This is where you begin to know what your version of

success looks like. Knowing how to grow, develop, and progress in your current role, company, and industry is critical to the success of your game plan.

4. **Design and work on your personal brand each day.** Think more about how people feel and connect with you. Develop close business relationships with your direct team and build a network across the company. Your success is determined as much, if not more, by how people think of you, how they feel about you, and if they really like you than by what you have done. Your brand tells others what they can expect from you. When you deliver (or better, overdeliver) against your brand, it reinforces that reputation. Just like with a product or service, people love and buy into brands.

5. **Learn the processes within your organization and who to go to when you need assistance or guidance.** Have a grasp of the rules and know which ones can be bent or broken to create significant positive impact. If you know who to go to, how to work with them and when, you become the person others go to for help. You can become extremely valuable in the organization by knowing how things work and being the lynchpin for connecting people to one another in the process.

6. **Become an expert on the business, the customer, the market, and the competition.** Learn what to do when unexpected problems arise. Everybody is good when things are good. Only standouts, however, excel when things become challenging. You want to be known as the person who knows the most and can solve problems. Again, the more you know, the more you grow.

The more problems you solve, the more value you get in return.

7. **Expand and enhance your network.** Align with people who can help you the most and reduce or eliminate the time you spend with those who drag you down. Help others to achieve their goals and become successful as well. Just like in school, use the full range of your network and be within the key network for others. You never know when a particular connection will lead to something unexpected.

8. **Seek and execute a few quick wins as soon as possible.** Establish yourself as a go-to person for projects that align with your strengths. When you deliver early and often, you establish your brand. You become known as the person who gets things done and you build a wealth of trust and responsibility.

9. **Ask a lot of questions and get as much feedback as possible.** Getting answers and acquiring knowledge about your performance are excellent learning tools. Leverage them wisely to create optimal odds for future success. More important than asking lots of questions is to ask the right questions. The most successful people ask the best questions and therefore, they get the best and most important information to make effective decisions, develop strategies, solve problems, and get things done. The better your inputs, the better your outputs.

10. **Continue to invest in yourself (ongoing professional development) and build/enhance your skills.** Learning doesn't end after graduation. To remain relevant and

impactful requires a lifelong love of learning. Growth and development comprise the upward rising journey in the decision tree of life. This is one of the other great separators for success and happiness.

THE IMPACT OF EARLY FOUNDATIONAL DECISIONS

It's important to restate a key idea. Your first or second (or possibly even your third) job won't be the make or break decisions that many people think they are. You can make a change at any time. Remember where you are on the football field of life. If you're in your early to mid-twenties, for example, you still have forty or more years to work, so the first four to six years are only 10-15 percent of your working life.

These entry-level positions are a time of learning, growing, and continuing to build your foundation. During this time, you have an opportunity to test drive new roles, skills, and industries to find out what you like and don't like, what you're good at, and not good at, where you can make a significant contribution, and where you can't. Use this time to build your skills and acquire new ones.

This is also a perfect time to develop your network, gain industry, customer, and professional knowledge, develop yourself personally, build your holistic success model, and leave a positive imprint on the jobs and people you leave behind. These jobs are not life or death. Rather, they're early opportunities in the game of life.

Each brick you place and hold together with another brick eventually becomes a layer of the foundation. You then build on top of that foundation with the next layer and then again, the next layer.

The important thing to remember is that what you do before college, university, or trade school becomes the foundation for that level. What you do in school becomes the foundation for your job or jobs. The jobs you take eventually help determine your life. The culmination of all that becomes your legacy.

BUILD FOUNDATIONS
Lay One Brick at a Time

LEGACY

IN LIFE
Holistic Planning and Actions

ON THE JOB
First 90 Days, 1–3 Year Goals, Career Plan

IN SCHOOL
Learn, Practice, Develop, Experience

BEFORE SCHOOL
Natural Gifts and Prior Foundations

It's important to realize that you can start to lay your bricks anywhere. It doesn't matter if you don't get that dream job or get into that first-choice school. If one of those goals doesn't work out, take your bricks and start to build your foundation somewhere else. You can still rise high, and the outcome might be even better.

If you need help on making an important job or career decision, think about a simple 20-60-20 rule. Approximately 20 percent of the job will suck but is essential for getting the job done. Meanwhile, 60 percent will be the day-to-day routine work that is neither good nor bad. The remaining 20 percent are the parts of the job you enjoy. These are the situations you prepare for and would do even if you didn't get paid. Don't take a job that is 80-10-10 or 60-35-5. You want an appropriate balance in your job that keeps you motivated, energized, and excited about what you're doing and what's coming next. Ideally, you'll find a job that feels more like 10-10-80!

Also, think about what you will get beyond money, titles, and other societal benchmarks for success. Think about how a job or career decision fits in your journey. Suppose you get offered a job at a large investment bank, make a lot of money, and develop skills related to finance, trading, and investing. If you choose an alternate path and work for a small company, you might learn a variety of things and gain broader experiences in operations, marketing, supply chain, customer experience, and technology. You won't necessarily go wrong either way, but if your ideal future is to be a CEO, you know which role to take as the foundation to your future.

YOUR CIRCLES OF LIFE

One of the most important foundations you can build is known as your *circles of life*. These are the people, information, and things surrounding you that will determine who you are, what you become, and what you will be able to accomplish in the future.

Life is a series of concentric circles with each one radiating outward in all different directions with you at the center. You have different circles for different parts of your life, and each one connects to and layers on top of the others to form a bonding and strengthening effect around your core.

The closer a circle is to your core, the more important the people or things in that circle are to your happiness and success. These circles should be given the highest priority in your life.

The further the circle is from your core, the less time, energy, and resources should be devoted to it. Anything outside your circle should be ignored and never let in.

If one circle isn't congruent with the others, you will feel the stress and impact on the other circles. The more congruent the circles, the more you start to build a tightly bonded 3D sphere around you and the stronger your core will be.

DUNBAR'S NUMBER

In relationships, there is a cognitive limit to the number of people you can have a stable and effective social relationship with. This is known as Dunbar's number, which suggests that there is a limit to the number of people you can maintain a stable social relationship with and can consider part of your ongoing social network. You only need five close or intimate relationships, fifteen good friends, and at most 150 acquaintances.

Acquaintances are people you can reach out to for help. They're more important than strangers, but not nearly as important as your inner circle. Your inner circle consists of the five people you spend the most time with. These are the people who have the most impact on who you are.

The closer a person is to your circle, the more impact they will have. The further out a person is to your circle, the less relevant they are. This is an important distinction, and it's the primary reason why you shouldn't let the words, actions, or opinions of your outer circle break into your circle and impact you at the core. If you do, that becomes your inner circle, which will radiate outward to your environment. Your closest circles will feel this effect the most.

STRENGTHENING YOUR CIRCLES

Your various circles are all around you and they relate to everything in your life, whether it's information you take in, the work on which you choose to focus, or the environment around you. If, for instance, you choose to predominantly watch the local or national news instead of reading a book, the constant drama of unfolding current events will take residence in your inner circle and have significant impact on you. However, the stronger and tighter your circles, the more you can deflect things and the more you can draw strength from what's closest to you.

For example, with a strong intimate relationship circle, you can deflect other interests and draw strength from your significant other. With the right books, podcasts, and other learning opportunities in your inner circle, you won't have time for other mindless and potentially destructive inputs. If you aren't inspired, supported, and strengthened by your circles, it's either time to get a new one or adjust those you already have.

To help understand and strengthen your circles of life, ask yourself the following questions that focus on the most critical circles and the inner and outer rings of each (but don't ignore your other life circles).

- **Personal relationships.** Who are the four or five people that form my closest relationships (inner circle)? Who are the one-time connections I need to maintain (outer circle)? Who do I need to remove from my circle altogether?
- **Work relationships.** Who are the four or five people that I associate with most at work to help my growth, development, and career (inner circle)? Who are the one-time connections I need to network with or go to for help (outer circle)?
- **Health.** Which physical activities and nutrition should I commit to every day (inner circle)? What are my guilty pleasures that I can indulge in once in a while (outer circle)? Which habits should I remove from my circle completely?
- **Learning.** Which authors, books, podcasts, or other resources do I go to the most (inner circle)? What resources do I use occasionally (outer circle)? Which resources should I ignore completely and push outside my circle?
- **Goals.** Which two or three goals matter the most to me (inner circle)? What goals are further out from the center (important but a lower priority)?
- **Projects.** What are the two or three key projects that would have the greatest impact on my career or goals (inner circle)? Which projects should I push to an outer circle? Are there any projects I should remove or delegate to someone else?

As part of your foundations work, be sure to identify each of your personal circles. Work to establish and strengthen them from the inside out. Protect and preserve them at all costs. This forms the all-important sphere of life around you and is a critical core element of your standout playbook.

ESTABLISHING A DAILY ROUTINE

Just as important as knowing what to do in the bigger picture of your life, school, work, and the circles around you is the ability to establish and maintain a successful daily routine. After all, your days are your life in miniature and the sum of all your days becomes your life. If you want a great life, live great days. The daily routine that you establish now will become the foundation for success later. You achieve positive results based on what you do consistently, not what you do every once-in-a-while.

There is no magic formula for establishing a daily routine. The key is to build one that creates structure and processes that enable you to live well. If you don't own and control your life, you'll wake up, check your emails, and spend your day reacting to everyone else's lives. Instead of chasing your own goals and dreams, you will be helping others chase theirs.

Having an established and effective daily routine also helps with balance. By owning and scheduling your day, you can do the things that are most important to you. You'll make progress toward your goals and dreams, while also allowing for other critical aspects to your happiness, such as engaging in healthy activities, spending time with loved ones, and having uninterrupted hours to work on key projects.

A common misconception is that people don't have time to do the things that they want to do during the day. The reality is that everyone has the time, but standouts prioritize and schedule what's important to them.

Once you identify what's important to you, build a daily schedule with your key priorities, including specific times that work best for you. The more routine your schedule, the more motivated you will be to stick with it.

For some people, waking up every day at 5:00 am is the best way to start their day. It gives them the time they need to fully awaken with a cup of coffee, invest in themselves by reading a book or listening to a podcast, working out at the gym, or going for a run and then preparing for their day before anyone else gets up. For some, this works with tremendous results.

What time should you wake up in the morning to be at your best every day? I can't tell you, because I'm not you. You might not even know what time works best for you...yet. The only surefire method to discovering that is to experiment, which is one of the guiding principles of being a standout.

The simple decision about when to wake up in the morning could be your first choice in establishing a daily routine that enables you to be at your best. Try waking up at 5:00 am one day, 6:00 am another. Maybe 9:00 am is the time that works best for you. The only way to find out is to try different times over a set period. Evaluate what worked and what didn't, and adjust accordingly.

If you have more energy at night, schedule your priorities in the evening. What matters most is that you have a schedule and follow it. The more you schedule, the more you do. The more you do, the higher you rise. The more you rise, the more you separate yourself from the rest.

Doing nothing or leaving your day to chance is the worst thing you can do. Research has shown that if you look at someone's calendar, you'll be able to see into their future (at least in general terms).

What you choose to focus on and do will determine how productive, meaningful, and satisfied you feel at the end of the day. From *The 7 Habits of Highly Effective People* written by Stephen R. Covey, prioritize, focus on, and do the things right now that are important and urgent. Plan later for the things that are important but not urgent. Delegate the things that appear to be urgent but aren't important, and drop the things that are neither urgent nor important.

The more your today fits into the upper left quadrant and your tomorrow fits into the upper right quadrant, the more control you will have over your daily routine, and the more you will move towards your goals and future vision.

Standouts focus on the things that are most important to them, not the unnecessary busy work and so-called *urgent* unimportant things that cause stress, anxiety, and a lack of balance. They plan and use their time more wisely and have key strategies around those plans and time to optimize their day. Standouts have the right supportive partner, focus on their goals, combine activities, set deadlines, and control their day (and therefore their life) to provide balance. Own your day or your day will own you.

Finally, time is the one resource that we all have that is exactly the same no matter who you are, where you live, or what you do. If you sleep fifty-six hours a week (eight hours a day) and work fifty-six hours a week (roughly five, eleven-hour days including travel), you will have fifty-six hours left in the week. This is another one of the great separators. Standouts use this "free" time more wisely, get more from their fifty-six-hour workweeks, and optimize their sleep better than the rest.

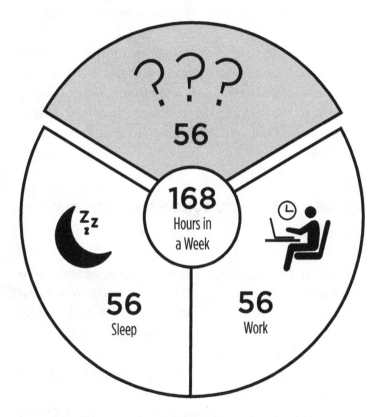

It's of extreme importance to realize that the suggestions expressed in this chapter are only ideas; they're not the be-all, end-all. As I've mentioned before, there is no *one*

way to success and happiness. Fortunately, there are an abundance of paths to those ideal destinations. You have to discover which ones work for you.

It's also extremely important to understand and build the foundations of your life. Like structural foundations, they serve as the load-bearing building blocks for what comes on top of it. Foundations provide an anchor against ever-changing external forces, and foundations prevent erosion that might come from underground, below what is seen.

Once you build your foundations including your daily routines, the people around you, what you know and are good at, and your safety nets and other elements, you're ready to start layering in the various floors of success that hopefully lead to beautiful, high-rise structures that we will all admire.

STAIRS TO HELP YOU BUILD YOUR FOUNDATIONS

Today:

- List all the basic things you need to do (resumes, practice interviews, business attire, core expectations of your job). These are the "table stakes" that everyone will do. Make sure you check them off but do them differently and exceed expectations.
- Evaluate your own personal 10-10-10 and identify the things you can do to be above the basics.
- Build and optimize your exterior support (the team around you, environment, network, key resources, daily habits, and other items).
- Develop your key plans [budget, financial future, health,

learning, career, contingency planning (when things go wrong), social media/marketing branding].

- Schedule your ideal day to do the most important things that move you forward. Eliminate the rest.

Every day:

- Did you probe, experiment, or take a risk to get out of your comfort zone, learn, and/or grow?
- Did you move the needle on building your foundations (connect with a key contact, check in with your team, build or refine your plans)?
- Did you do the hard thing, prepare and practice for a future game time (key event, opportunity, defining moment)?
- Did you move closer to perfect by gaining knowledge, getting better at your craft, honing your skill, preparing for your defining moment?
- Review how you performed against your schedule and build a better, more effective schedule tomorrow. Have a preliminary schedule for the week, month, and quarter. The more you plan ahead, the better your chances of success in that future.

Main goal: Build your plans, operating procedures, and optimal environment for tomorrow. Lay the foundations for future success now.

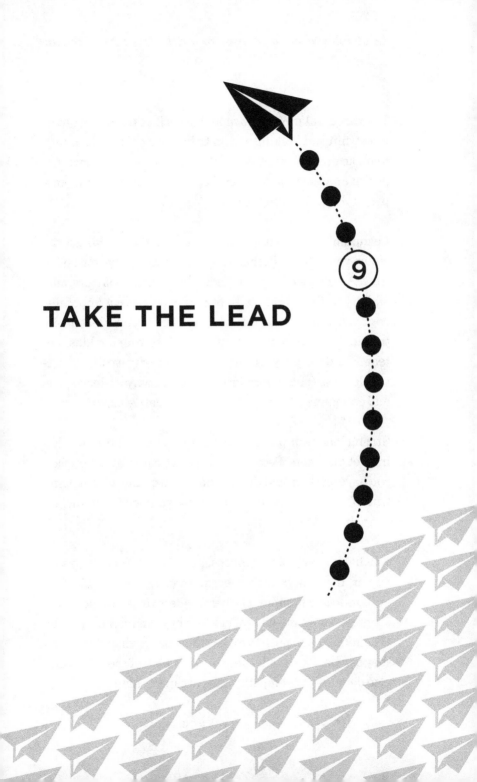

TAKE THE LEAD

"Leadership is not a position or a title, it is action and an example."

~COREY BOOKER

The three-pillar purpose model describes the importance of learning and taking action to be your best self, leading to make others better, and making a difference by having a positive and significant impact on others. These are the core principles of standing out.

Leadership, like being a standout, is not something with which you're born. Rather, it is something you become over time. As you develop your leadership traits, behaviors, and skills, you share them with others in a way that hopefully connects them to that experience. They become leaders in the mold that you demonstrated. This is true for our kids, our teams, and the people around us. That's why we follow certain leaders (positive experiences), and why we leave jobs and companies due to poor leaders (negative experiences).

Strong leadership is an action and a feeling that has an impact on others. People follow you because of the impact you have on them and the emotions you create within them. One of the best questions you can ask yourself is whether or not you would follow you.

The best leaders aren't necessarily those in positions of power. Instead, they connect with us as people. They're authentic and humble. The best leaders respect others and are great communicators. They lead by example, hold people accountable, and push to make others better than they think they can be. The best leaders have a vision of the future but also demonstrate empathy and care in the moment.

Simon Sinek says, "A boss has the title, but a leader has the people." We follow leaders who move our emotions, care about us, inspire us to be our best, and help us get things done the right way.

This process of creating a great leader involves a decision-tree type of journey, where you make choices in a step-by-step fashion to grow and develop. That journey involves learning about leadership, discovering your unique leadership style, practicing, perfecting, and ultimately exemplifying your leadership brand and image.

A Google search for leadership books yields more than fifty million results. You could spend your life learning about and practicing leadership, which is good advice by the way. This chapter provides you with two key frameworks on leadership as part of the overall standout playbook. It is your responsibility, however, to take the journey, learn about your unique leadership in detail, practice being the leader you want to be, and exemplify that leadership vision.

FIVE LEADERSHIP TYPES

Everybody wants to follow a leader. People look to others for inspiration, guiding wisdom, and confidence to move in certain directions. This is a curious aspect of human nature. We seek the strength of others to show us the way forward.

Acclaimed American author, motivational speaker, and leadership guru John Maxwell has given many speeches, written numerous books, and provided tremendous insight into the holistic view of leadership. One of his greatest philosophies—in my opinion—revolves around the way he articulates five types of leadership. Some of these you may recognize quickly while others you might have overlooked.

TITLE (POSITION RIGHT)

The most obvious type of leadership is title. Title is a basic leadership role where people follow you, not necessarily because they want to, but because they must because of your position. In most cases, they have a simple choice, which is to either follow your direction or find another job.

This type of leadership can be dangerous because it can appear unwarranted. In the hands of the insufficiently trained and self-unaware individual, leadership based on title alone can actually produce detrimental results for everyone involved. This is why some people remain managers and not leaders when given a title as leadership.

A Standout leader recognizes roles and authority, but they don't ever use that to gain leadership power. They use it only after they listen to others, and they simply make a decision because that's their role.

RELATIONSHIP (PERMISSION RIGHT)

People will also follow an individual they like as a person. When someone admires something about you—perhaps it's your emotional intelligence, performance under pressure, or the way you actively listen—they become drawn to you. There are limitless ways that inspire others to follow you. It may simply be that you have a good sense of humor or have a uniquely wonderful sense of fashion.

Once you discover what it is about you that makes people like you, leverage those qualities to lead. People don't follow you because they have to but because they want to. They believe in you and trust you, so they grant you the permission to lead them.

RESULTS (PRODUCTION RIGHT)

If you gain a reputation for getting things done, people will go to you when they need results. Others will follow you because of what you have done for the organization.

Think about Kobe Bryant. He scored a lot of points, played great defense, and won championships. Teammates, fans, and others followed him because of the production he achieved in his chosen craft.

This form of leadership isn't relegated to professional athletes. The business world is anchored by producers. This shouldn't be confused with the first type of leadership, which exclusively concerns title. That can be achieved by anyone with a name on their office door.

The producer-based leader could be an intern in the mailroom. If that person knows how to get rush deliveries out on time, every time, regardless of extenuating circumstances, people will look to them for guidance on how to get the job done. An intern with such qualities will likely grow their leadership easily and have great potential to achieve much more.

DEVELOPMENT (PEOPLE RIGHT)

This is another type of results-oriented leadership, but its focus is on what you do for other people, not the organization. We all occasionally ask the question, "What can you do for me?" We follow leaders that have our best interest in mind and help us to achieve the goals and dreams we have for ourselves. These are the leaders who deeply care about the people who work for them. They invest in their people by helping them to get promoted, enhancing and developing their skills, providing challenging work, and fostering their growth.

When we work for leaders who are people-results oriented, we want to stay on their team. We feel a higher sense of job satisfaction with leaders like them. When we see people-results-oriented leaders in other areas, we desire to work for those teams. We seek mentors that can help us achieve certain things and remember teachers who helped us learn something new or get good grades.

Similarly, we play harder for captains on teams that make us elevate our game and achieve higher levels of performance. We seek coaches, tutors, peers, and others who see the potential in us, and we're motivated and inspired by people who give their time, energy, and talents to help us grow and become more than we think we can be.

Leadership is about people, and the more you can positively impact and help others, the more you will be considered a leader. A good leader motivates and helps people go to where they want to go. A great leader inspires people to go where they need to be or should be.

VISION AND VALUE (RESPECT RIGHT)

The highest level of leaders are people we follow because of who they are, what they represent, and what they value. This could be someone you know, but many times it's someone you've never met.

Whether it's Elon Musk or Bob Iger, Richard Branson, or anyone else, we follow people we admire, those who share our personal values, or people who represent an idea of who we want to be. We get behind them because we believe in them, and we respect who they are, not what they are.

This one could easily be misinterpreted as *a natural born leader,* but that's not the case. People aren't given respect by default. Respect is something that has to be earned through thoughts, words, and actions.

The people who become leaders based on the respect they get from others are made through their own impact on the people around them. More specifically, they represent a culmination of all the other leadership types.

Although title is likely the least important of these types, some people have a title that declares them a leader, but they also back it up by fostering great relationships, producing eye-catching results, and developing people.

Standout leaders garner respect from others by assuming all these leadership types. This type of leader has the ability to create massive, positive change for themselves, their community, and the world around them.

THE LEADERSHIP JOURNEY

To become a great leader, you need to start by knowing that

you're a leader now, regardless of title or whether or not you think it's in your DNA. Understand that leadership is within you, but now you need to grow that ability. Then you can help others to get better and have significant positive impact in the world.

The Center for Creative Leadership (CCL) is an organization I have attended at various points in my professional life. CCL provides an environment optimized for learning about leadership and creating success at work as well as in life.

They use a model that aligns well with the three-pillar purpose model I've outlined in this book. This model also does a great job of depicting the leadership journey I recommend as part of the Standout Experience.

LEADING YOURSELF

Notice the first phase of the CCL's model for leadership is aptly titled, *self.* As I stated earlier, this is how your leadership journey begins. You learn as much about yourself as possible.

In this first phase, you discover what your career competencies are—what you like and don't like, as well as what you're great at, and not great at. This is also where you dive deeply into your emotional intelligence and the social skills that will help you to accomplish your goals and achieve your unique vision of success.

In Centered Leadership, you find ways to motivate, inspire, and lead yourself to bigger and better things. This is not only the hardest form of leadership, it's also the most overlooked.

In leading yourself, you develop and grow your skills, business knowledge, self-power, and social impacts. You work on and enhance your emotional intelligence to become more self-aware and demonstrate more self-control. Likewise, you also develop social awareness and social control. This is where you build core competencies around learning ability, influence, communication, empathy, and results-driven actions. If you can lead yourself and push past your own limitations, comfort zone, and current state, you can do the same for others.

LEADING OTHERS

Only when you fully learn how to lead yourself, will you be able to lead others; not manage, but lead them. In this phase, you'll leverage your ability to empathize and communicate with others to drive results. That is where the discovery process of emotional intelligence from the centered phase of your leadership journey will be of great value.

Relational leadership is when someone brings a group of people together in an attempt to accomplish something or make a difference in the interest of the common good. This form of leadership involves empowerment, inclusion, purposefulness, and ethical group behavior.

This type of leadership could be in a one-to-one setting or one-to-many, but it starts with a genuine interest in others, and forms a personal connection that makes the person being mentored feel like they're the only one in the room. These powerful leaders are humble, approachable, and they're generous with their time, talents, and energy for the good of others.

Relational leaders are authentic and demonstrate empathy, but they're also willing to push someone past the point of where they think they can go. This serves the first pillar of the purpose model, embodies the second, and is a key component of the third pillar, which is all about making a difference.

LEADING LEADERS

From leading others comes your ability to lead leaders. Think of this as a second-level management position within a company. Team leaders might have a group of ten or twelve people under their direct scope of management, but they also likely have a manager above them in the organizational hierarchy that directs them.

Leaders of leaders integrate across functional areas more than leaders of individuals. Because of their roles, they handle more complexity and implement more goals, strategies, and tactics that get pushed through the leaders of individuals. Leaders of leaders set standards, hold their managers to higher expectations, and clear the way for other leaders and their teams to do their job well. They drive more results and think and act more systematically in the organization. These leaders are also better at recognizing and assisting future leaders of leaders so they can take the reins from them when they're ready. Leaders of leaders also don't necessarily delegate, but they will when they have to. Mostly, they empower and help focus leaders and managers on the things that are most important.

LEADING FUNCTIONS

After you learn how to lead other people and lead leaders, you can lead functions.

In any organization, you might achieve a point in your leadership journey where you lead a department, such as human resources, finance, procurement, or any other area business unit. Leading a function means you're leading a larger group of people, which is why the first three forms of leadership are an important foundation.

This is a point in the journey that may come a little farther down the road in your career path. Standouts will likely hit this point much more quickly than their peers because they'll know how to leverage all of their unique strengths to move up the organizational hierarchy without getting stalled at any particular area.

Becoming a leader of functions is an achievement worth detailed inspection. At this point, you'll have the ability to affect how departments are run, which will shape the direction of an entire organization. You focus heavily on goals, strategies, and tactics and use KPIs (Key Performance Indicators) to measure your success more routinely than other leaders. With a heavy focus on getting things done on time, on budget, and on strategy, you will build a reputation for being someone who drives results.

This is where leaders in the organization put most of their weight and value and it's where success is sensed by most people. If you don't embody the previous roles of standout leadership, you won't remain here for long. The combination of all of these levels is how you move from good to great.

LEADING ORGANIZATIONS

Think about the leadership journey in terms of a career path.

As an employee of an organization, you're likely leading yourself. Through hard work, determination, and by producing consistently excellent results, you'll get the opportunity to lead others. If you excel in your leadership role of others, you might advance to the next level, where you lead a leader. From there, you might become a department head, and ultimately lead the entire business as a CEO or whatever it is that represents the highest role within the organization.

As a leader of organizations, you will not only have the ability to shape the way the business is executed and lead the company to your vision, but you could impact the way the entire industry and even the world works.

Think about some of the great leaders of organizations, like Bill Gates, Sheryl Sandberg, and Elon Musk. They are changing history with their vision. As a leader of an organization, you will have the chance for that same impact.

LEADERSHIP IN ACTION

It's true that great leaders are made, not born. A key distinction to that truth, however, is that everyone has some form of innate leadership, but that doesn't mean that everyone is a leader.

You have to work and grow into a leadership level. Leadership is something you do, not something you are. Some people are happy being followers and will only grow to be a manager. A big part of being a standout leader, however, is growing that innate leadership to achieve your full potential, getting extraordinary achievements out of ordinary people, and having maximum impact.

People want to get behind great leaders and be around someone they trust to inspire, assist, and guide them. Depending on where you're at in life, people are already looking to you for leadership in ways you might not recognize.

- If you have children, they're looking up to you as a role model for how they should behave in life's key situations.
- If you have people reporting to you in a work capacity, they're trying to emulate your work ethic and how you meet the demands of the business.
- If you're a high-performing student, your peers may be watching how you study for exams and the work you put into school.
- If you're widely respected in the community, young people may grow into adulthood with the same altruistic mindset because of your positive output on them.

Those reasons are why you should realize that leadership is already within you and you're knowingly or unknowingly exhibiting it. Now, it's your time to grow that potential, develop your leadership style, and stand out as not just a leader but an elite leader. In this way, you can have tremendous impact on the world, which represents the third pillar of the three-pillar purpose model.

While this is a short chapter on leadership, the overall book is essentially a model and a playbook for leadership. First and foremost, this is your leadership journey and you must own it and create it yourself while getting help along the way.

You will become a better leader if you're the authentic (and best) you. People love to follow greatness and they look to great leaders as examples of who they want to be. As any great leader does, you must have a vision of the future for them and the organization. You must also inspire everyone to work toward that future and ultimately impact others and make a difference in the world.

What kind of leader do you want to be and why? What is the result of you becoming a great leader? How will your leadership style be felt by others?

Once you know where you are and where you want to go, you need to learn and grow into a leader. You need to prepare, think, and act like a leader. Standouts set the standard for what leadership looks like in their company, school, or community.

As you learn and grow, you will also practice, practice, practice your leadership and build the foundations for you to be a great leader through knowledge, wisdom, core values, key skills, results, and experience.

Another key factor in being a standout leader is that you not only stand out when things are good but more importantly, you become an even greater leader when things don't go so well or there is a major problem or crisis.

Anyone can lead when you have great employees and things are going well. A standout leader is a versatile athlete. They recognize what is needed in the moment and rise to the occasion. You can feel their leadership in the moments you look to them for guidance, wisdom, and direction.

As you become a standout leader, you will exude optimism, generate a positive energy, and demonstrate courage, curiosity, and integrity. Most importantly, you will stand out in the moments that matter most, because you're prepared and able to rise to the challenge. You will approach each day on a relentless pursuit of your leadership capability, and you will make sure that your impact on others lasts well beyond your physical presence and time with them. As Stephen Covey says, "What you do (as a leader) has far greater impact than what you say."

STAIRS TO HELP YOU TAKE THE LEAD

Today:

- Identify ways that you lead yourself and how you can be a better self-leader.
- Sign up for leadership development training and build an ongoing leadership development growth plan.
- Identify the leaders you admire most. What qualities, values, and leadership styles do you like best and how can you emulate them?
- Determine the type of leader you want to be for others. Do the research to learn about all the key qualities that make a great leader, and know the difference between a leader and a manager.
- Assume a leadership role in your function, school, group, or area.

Every day:

- Reflect on a leadership lesson you learned today. What leadership values did you apply today?
- Examine the ways you grew as a leader through enhanced knowledge or skills. Read a chapter from a leadership book, listen to a leadership podcast, or learn from another leader or resource.

- What opportunity do you have tomorrow to demonstrate your leadership skills (key decisions, teaching others, communicating effectively, getting more from your team, asking questions, providing feedback, leading by example)?
- Reflect on your leadership today. What can you do better? Is your team working on the right things? What was the outcome of your leadership today?
- Did you demonstrate your leadership in all areas of your life today? How else can you grade yourself today and prepare to shine your leadership value tomorrow?

Main goal: Know your leadership style and how you can play a leadership role.

MAKE AN IMPACT

10

"I can tell you from experience, the effect you have on others is the most valuable currency there is."

~JIM CARREY

Who you are, what you do, and how you lead culminates in the impact you have on other people and the world. You decide if that impact is positive or negative. Either way, the difference you make might be big or small, temporary or long term, but whatever the outcome, you will make a difference, and you definitely matter.

Your legacy will be determined by the effect you have on others. It won't be determined by what happens to you and for you, it will be determined by what happens from you and because of you.

Albert Einstein once said that we should not strive to be a person of success, but instead we should work hard to be a person of impact. Our heroes and the people we admire most are not looked up to because of their fame, money, or titles. Rather, we look up to them, want to be like them, and we remember them for their impact on others.

We might not rise to the fame and fortune of people like Einstein, Edison, Elon Musk, Bill Gates, Oprah, or anyone else that comes to mind. Perhaps only our immediate family and friends, children, and inner circle of people will feel and be better because of our impact. Even one life is worth impacting, however, just as your life is worth being impacted by someone else.

The more people, places, and things that you positively impact because of who you are, what you do, and how you do it, the more you will be recognized for making a difference in the world and the greater your legacy will be. Your success, value, and net worth will be determined by the number of people you positively impact.

Standing out comes down to these last three chapters. All of the knowledge gained and work you put in from the earlier chapters sets the stage and creates the opportunities for you to shine for others. This is where your private efforts become public value.

The more you do for yourself, the more you'll be able to do for others.

The more impact you have on others, the more you will stand out.

The more you stand out, the more you'll get in return.

The more you get in return, the more you can reinvest into yourself and your mission.

The more you reinvest, the more positively you will compound the cycle.

Keep in mind that standing out is about being uniquely you and doing things differently than the rest. You will never impact and influence the world if you are just like it.

THE IMPACT OF MAKING AN IMPACT

In the previous chapter, you learned that great leaders are made, not born. They don't set out to be a leader, but they do set out to make a difference. It's true that nobody is born a leader, but we're all born to contribute in our own way. Regardless of where you came from or who you are, you have the ability to affect and be affected by others.

Furthermore, understand that no act of kindness, happiness, or love is ignored or wasted. You don't have to be perfect or do something big to make a difference; you just have to care and be present in the moment. Some acts of kindness may take a second to perform, but for the recipient, the impact may last a lifetime.

Whether you realize it or not, you're chosen for a job, a spouse or life partner, or anything else because of the impact you have or will have. It's not only about being able to do the job or fulfill a particular role. You're chosen because of what you can do in that role.

People and businesses really want to know what you will do for them, whether they admit it or not. We're self-serving creatures who strive for survival, belonging, and happiness. We choose others who can help us, make our lives better, and make a positive contribution to our organizations.

DO THE MATH

Most of us have more impact than we realize. Simple math would suggest that if you live for eighty years and have an effect on at least two people every day, that equates to almost 60,000 opportunities to create positive impact in your lifetime! Don't ever think that you don't make a difference or can't have an impact.

An article published in *Psychology Today* by Tim Elmore suggests that even the world's biggest introverts will influence at least 10,000 people in a lifetime. Imagine how many people you have knowingly and unknowingly influenced in your life *so far*. There is no question that your presence in this world will have some impact on others, even if it's just a few. So, why not make that impact as meaningful as possible, or at least enjoy trying?

Every person you come in contact with is impacted in some way. Something as seemingly insignificant as a smile or an unexpected compliment has the potential to stick with someone all day, but you could also do something extraordinary today that impacts thousands or even millions of people.

Just by being in a particular place at a particular time has an impact. Leaving work one late summer evening, a car was trying to get in front of me at a traffic light and I let it go. She was the last person to go through the light and she sped through just in time.

At that very moment, a large, all-white warehouse delivery truck came speeding through the intersection completely unaware of the traffic signals. Had I gone through the light instead of letting the other car speed past me, I might have been hit squarely on the driver's side, and there is no telling what might have happened. In some way, that seemingly inconsequential act of taking up space might have saved my life.

The point is that everything you say, every action you take, and the overall experience of you is a potentially powerful input for someone else psychologically, emotionally, spiritually, or even physically.

HOW TO MAKE AN IMPACT

Now that you know you do make a difference and you have impact, the question becomes...*How do you make a difference in the world and stand out in the lives of others?*

Start by changing yourself. Just like leadership begins from the inside, so does impact. As Mother Theresa told us, "The world would be a cleaner and better place if we all just swept our own doorstep." By changing who you are, what you do, and how you do it, you will by default change how other people see and feel you.

Next, realize that impact is not relative to time. Some moments of impact are immediate; others may take years to materialize and reach their full potential. Those longer-term impacts, however, also have the ability to create a lasting effect, capable of contributing substantially to an ongoing legacy. The more you approach each day with the intention to have impact, the more likely you are to actually do it.

Finally, knowing how to make an impact involves realizing that it does not need to be something monumental. All you have to do is recognize the opportunity and start right away. You don't know what the other person is feeling or going through. Therefore, even the smallest act of kindness, caring, love, help, or support could go a long way. You don't have to impact the world. Sometimes, all you need to do is impact one person's world.

I remember having a conversation with my brother one night after Thanksgiving dinner. He just left his job working for a local resort in Orlando and after spending years working for a few prominent luxury brands, he wondered where his career was going and what he would do in the long term.

We spent time talking about his love for sports as we were watching one of the evening football games. Maybe it was the wine or maybe it was something else, but I looked at him and asked the question, "What if?"

What if he went back to school and followed his love for sports? What if he started at the local community college, focused on getting into one of the larger state schools, worked for the athletic department, and pursued his career in sports management or sports marketing?

Flash forward a few years, and not only did he graduate (credit to him for taking the necessary steps to pursue his dreams), but he's now working in his dream job for his dream university. One simple conversation led to a life-altering decision.

I can tell you from experience that inspiring and helping others to do more and be more is one of the most rewarding things you can do. It's also how you start to make an impact one conversation and one person at a time.

Later, you can scale your impact (what you do and how you do it) through your acquired skills, job, scope of responsibility, the products, services, and experiences you offer, and so on. The greater your scale of impact, the greater your success and happiness in life.

Standouts create impact by going beyond the *golden rule*, which is to treat others the way you want to be treated. Instead, they're driven by the *platinum rule*, which is to treat others the way *they* want to be treated.

You can follow the platinum rule by truly understanding someone else and believing in them, encouraging them, challenging them, and supporting them. The idea is to pay it forward (give back what you have been given). The greatest gifts you can give to someone or something are your time, energy, resources, and support.

Have fun discovering new ways to challenge yourself every day to make impact.

DIFFERENCE-MAKING BEHAVIORS

People who work to make a difference exhibit certain behaviors that allow them to have impact. The more they invest in these behaviors, the greater the impact they have.

- They commit to the relentless pursuit of making themselves better (self-impact).
- They consistently help others and think of new ways to be of service.
- They enjoy the process of making a difference as a specific goal.
- They welcome and encourage others to help them in the journey.
- They commit their life to the mission of impact.
- Their key resources (time, energy, and talent) are used more for others than themselves.

- They set an inspiring example for others to model and follow.
- They operate from a place of love and deep caring for others.
- They have a meaningful and positive way of connecting with others.
- They pay good deeds forward.
- They are involved in the world and know the changes that need to happen.

Once you're fully in-tune with how these behaviors enable you to make a difference, you'll be ready to begin and ultimately master the process of having impact.

THE PROCESS OF HAVING AN IMPACT

Any new impactful idea, whether it's big or small, follows a process that begins with awareness of a certain problem or opportunity and ends with the leadership of enacting a potential solution and measuring the impact. Having an impact on others involves this same flow.

1. Become aware of the situation and understand why it needs to be addressed.

2. Develop potential solutions to the problem or opportunity.

3. Customize the best solution to suit the specific area of need.

4. Develop a strategic plan for implementation of the solution.

5. Execute the strategic plan.

6. Measure the impact of the solution.

7. Test and adjust as necessary.

8. Provide leadership that empowers others to take on maintenance of the solution.

This process is meant to serve as a general guideline. There is nothing absolute about it. The key is having better awareness, making critical decisions, and taking massive action.

Standouts are able to identify opportunities, no matter how big or how small. They can put a strategic plan together, inspire and recruit the best performers who can make it happen, and then lead others to take the necessary steps to see that plan into action. The elite standouts are also able to measure the success (or not) of the plan and actions and adjust as necessary.

You can follow these steps to help one person or a lot of people, to tackle a specific project or launch a new business opportunity. The idea is that you always have an opportunity to leave a footprint where you are on a person, a place, or a thing. There are opportunities all around you. The question is, are you up to the challenge?

THE EXPERIENCE OF YOU IS AN IMPACT

Similarities between implementing a business solution and having a positive impact in the world go beyond mere process. A great business idea is part of a larger experience related to the total brand. The same goes for the impact you have on others; it's related to the larger experience of you.

The impact you have on another person becomes an experience directly (or indirectly) associated with you. When these experiences are stacked on top of each other, it forms a full-scale model of how people think about you and perceive your personal brand. As you start to differentiate yourself from the crowd and create memorable, positive emotional experiences for others, you begin to stand out.

As an interesting comparison, consider something most of us consume every day—coffee. By using this comparison, you can clearly see how shifting from what everyone else does (a commodity) to fully differentiating yourself through experiences creates real value.

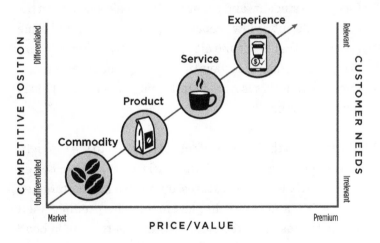

The bottom-left section of the associated diagram is the commodity. This is the raw material, where everything looks and feels the same.

No differentiating factors exist in a commodity. There is an abundance of resources to pull from and the opportunity to separate one from the other is unknown (blind) to the decision maker. Generally, the choice of a commodity comes down to a basic strategic choice like lowest cost or easiest to acquire.

Think about a coffee bean. There are lots of places to get beans and nothing separates one from the other (sometimes there are higher quality beans, but you get the point). In most cases, there is nothing especially impactful about the bean itself. For our purposes, this is akin to people going about their daily life without having any impact on others. This also equates to the basic skills, general requirements, core expectations, and standard processes that everyone has or goes through.

I see many students and young professionals focusing on the same skills, interview preparations, networking, and same processes that everyone else goes through. This is where everyone spends all of their time, energy, and resources not knowing that this is not the differentiating factor. This is only the commodity.

Moving from the bottom left of the diagram to the top right, the commodity becomes differentiated through a better-quality product, more features, unique packaging, targeted marketing, and strategic placement. The product itself starts to make a difference. This is how the coffee bean becomes the packaged coffee, and where different flavors, packaging, and brands start to separate.

Similarly, who you are, your experiences, skills, and what

you do is the product. It becomes differentiated from all the commoditized graduating students and young professionals when you can do it better than them. It becomes further differentiated when you combine multiple product offerings to add more value and have the versatility to add new products and features to what you offer.

Moving further up the value chain, some companies take the product (coffee) and extend its value by preparing and providing you with coffee. By shifting from the product itself to the act of preparing and serving the coffee elevates what stands out in your mind. Better service generally comes at a higher price, but also adds more value to the consumer. This fulfills the final part of the equation for most businesses, which is the *how*.

As an individual, you can further differentiate yourself by how you do or serve your unique offering. By providing the highest quality product and delivering it in a way that exceeds customer experiences, you stand out in the minds of others. Undoubtedly, people will begin to request your product and service. They will even be willing to pay more for it. In this model, the *how* you do things becomes a service, where the impact created is greater than the product itself.

Offering a product or service better than anyone else is still only part of the equation. Standouts turn that amazing product and service into an experience (like shifting from coffee beans, to coffee, to serving coffee, to the Starbucks experience).

Here, you not only offer a compelling product, but you have an exceptional service and deliver an experience on someone else when it matters most. You move people's emotions, give them value beyond what they thought they needed, connect with them, exceed all expectations, and offer more of the standout elements that will be discussed in the next chapter.

The Standout Experience of you happens when you know *what* to deliver, *when* to deliver it, *how* to deliver it, and you do it in a way that leaves a lasting, emotional experience for someone else.

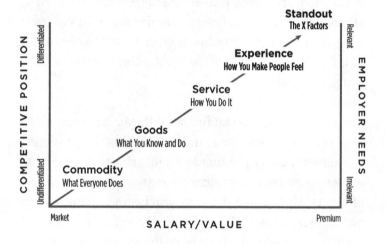

One of my favorite coaches at the Center for Creative Leadership in Colorado once challenged me with a notion that changed my life. He said, "You work for Disney, which creates these magical experiences for their guests. They transport people into an immersive and magical world, provide exceptional products and services, move emotions, and create lasting memories that bring them back repeatedly." Then he asked if I, as a Disney cast member, do the same thing.

When I asked what he meant, he said, "What is the Disney

experience of you? How do you immerse others into the transformational experience of you? How do you provide exceptional gifts and services that exceed expectations and move people's emotions to create lasting memories, while keeping them coming back for more?

This was a game changer!

People that stand out live for something bigger than themselves and they make a lasting impact on the time, space, and people around them. They don't end up simply visiting this world, they leave a mark for everyone to see and feel.

You too can make a difference and if you do, by default, you will stand out. The richness, significance, and legacy of your impact will determine the amount by which you separate yourself from the rest. If you're aware of the impact you have on others and commit to the intention of making an impact on one person or hundreds every day, you will stand out.

STAIRS TO HELP YOU MAKE AN IMPACT

Today:

- Write down everyone who has made an impact on you, whether you know them or not. What did they do to make a difference and how did they do it? What can you do to pay that forward in your own way?
- Think about some small or random acts of kindness that put a smile on your face. How can you do something similar for someone else? Occasionally, having an impact is when someone else sees you giving love and joy to others.
- Going back to your *ikigai*, write down various ways that

the world needs you and your talents. Ensure you're passionate about those ideas and capable of contributing in them. How would your contribution impact others?

- Decide how you will measure your impact on the world in the short term and in the long run. What does success and happiness look like to you, in terms of your impact?

Every day:

- Identify someone who needs your time, talents, and small act of kindness. How will that impact them today?
- Determine something you can change to make a process, product, service, or experience better today (or move this forward towards a goal end date).
- Consider the things that made an impact on you today.
- Think about how today was different because you were alive.

Main goal: Identify ways—now or in the future, big or small— you can make a difference in the world or in someone's life. This is your legacy.

GO STAND OUT

"Why fit in when you were born to stand out!?"

~DR. SEUSS

This is it—the big payoff.

Everything you've read and everything you've done to this point has led you to this moment. Your level of preparation and how your *ready state* self will perform in the moment will determine if you stand out.

The worst thing that can happen is that a standout moment arrives and you aren't ready. By the time it comes, it's too late. Even if you do everything perfectly, it doesn't always mean that you will stand out. Three factors must all come together at the right moment, at the right place, and in the right way:

- You have to be ready and deliver exactly what is needed in the way it needs to be delivered.
- The other person must be open and ready for what you deliver in your unique way.
- The environment around you must have the right conditions.

The challenge is that nobody can operate at the highest level all the time, which is one of the fallacies of peak performance. You're human, which means you're capable of doing amazing things, but it also indicates you'll occasionally fall short of your own expectations and those of the people around you. It also means that others have a lot going on in their own lives and they might not be in the right state of mind, the right emotional place, or the right situation that will allow you to stand out. Even if both of you are perfect in that place and in that moment, the conditions might not allow for the standout opportunity to occur. It's unrealistic to expect that you will always be at your peak, the other person will think, feel, and do exactly as you hoped, and the conditions will be perfect, every day.

People who stand out do so for the right people at the right time, even if they aren't at their peak. They're able to display their "A" game more often than others, but they also know how to be really good when they have only their "B" or "C" game available. More importantly, they understand that the world needs any game they can bring for a cause bigger than themselves.

In effect, standouts increase the opportunities and probabilities for success. They do what 98 percent of the rest won't do so that they are in the top 2 percent of whatever environment they are in. They stand out!

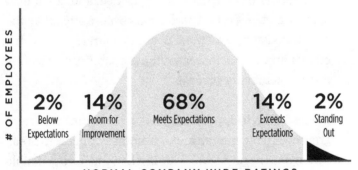

NORMAL COMPANY-WIDE RATINGS

WHAT DOES IT MEAN TO STAND OUT?

Standing out is not a singular, easy-to-define thing, and it's not reserved for only the special 2 percent of the population. We all have the opportunity to experience standing out in one of four ways, but each one is progressively harder to achieve. Each level also requires more effort, differentiation, and preparedness.

1. **Moment in Time.** These are the one-time events that happen in each of our lives. Some moments like graduations, weddings, and achieving a significant milestone or goal are planned and common to all of us. Other moments are unplanned and unique to individuals. Either way, these are the specific standout times that we all experience in our lives in different ways.

2. **Consistent Greatness.** The next level is available to all of us, but not everyone gets to experience it. This is when someone stands out because they are consistently better than others over a longer period of time. They leverage their unique talents, work harder than anyone else, deliver more than what is needed, and are able to achieve higher levels of performance more often than the rest. Consistent Greatness does not guarantee anything, but it significantly increases the probability of standing out and achieving success.

3. **Breakthrough Opportunity.** At some point, consistent greatness isn't enough and it becomes difficult to break through to the next level. This is when you have to double down on your playbook and work even harder, smarter, and better to push through the barrier. You can get there, but it will require more than what you are doing, and it may require doing something completely different. At this level, there are fewer opportunities and much more competition.

4. **Reaching the Peak**. This is the ultimate standout level that only a few will reach. Whether it's the CEO of a company, the head of a large division, or the MVP of a professional sports league, reaching the peak requires help and something beyond extraordinary. Often, there are a number of uncontrollable factors that determine who gets to this level. All you can do is put yourself in the best position to be the one chosen when the moment comes.

Regardless of the standout level, the first thing you must do is understand what you are striving for and why. From that point, you can determine how to do it and if you are willing to pay the price to make it happen.

HOW DOES SOMEONE STAND OUT?

To stand out means you get noticed for doing something that rises above the routine or goes well beyond the expectations of others. The most important factor to standing out is being different and doing something better than the rest. If you or something breaks the rhythmic chain, that will be a standout moment.

Think about doing or seeing the same thing every day. The minute someone or something interrupts that normal, it stands out and leaves an impression on your mind and often your emotions.

Your goal should be to create as many opportunities to stand out as possible. The more opportunities you create and capitalize on, the more successful your life will be. Recognize the routines and normal expectations all around you. Then, prepare and purposefully find ways to create that unique and impactful moment.

By doing a quick Google search, you'll find that most advice and suggestions for standing out for students and young professionals center around leveraging your strengths, doing excellent work, being a team player, getting to know the business, networking, etc. That standard advice is true, but those notions are also considered basic expectations to fulfill when you're hired to do any job. They're the reasons—or table stakes—you were hired in the first place.

By fulfilling the table stakes of an opportunity, you're simply doing the same thing as everyone else by meeting the basic expectations of others. Nothing about that approach makes you stand out. This concept is the heart of what this book is all about. It's an untapped school of thought that will prove undeniably helpful in your quest for answers about how to move forward past school and into a happy and successful life.

You must go beyond those *table stakes* (what is taught today and the basic expectations others have of you), rise above the rest, and become memorable to stand out.

WHY DO CERTAIN PEOPLE STAND OUT?

In the book *The Power of Moments,* authors Dan and Chip Heath provide interesting insight about how some situations are more impactful than others and how key moments exist within every opportunity. They use examples and research to back up four key observations—in particular—about what we remember:

- Moments that elevate above our normal expectations.
- Moments that create a sense of pride or accomplishment.
- Moments that provide a key insight or stunning realization (an *aha* moment).
- Moments that connect to a special meaning or emotion.

It's my firm belief that standing out as a person works very much in the same way.

Over the last twenty years or so, I've been fascinated with how certain people rise above the rest, why some are more impactful and inspirational than others, why certain people perform better when it matters most, and how I can do the same thing.

I've been most curious when I've seen others promoted before me, even when I thought I was the better candidate and had done everything that was asked of me.

After much consideration, I've come to realize that there was something extraordinary about the people who were chosen ahead of me. Furthermore, I now understand that being chosen takes much more than just hard work and getting things done.

To understand why and how certain people stand out, I've spent years collecting my own insights through observations and experiences. I've interviewed hundreds of leaders, high performers, recruiters, peers, experts in psychology and peak performance, and anyone else that I can learn from. I've read books, attended workshops and seminars, and listened to podcasts. I've even spent time watching and analyzing certain shows like *America's Got Talent*, *The Voice*, and

American Idol to try to figure out why certain performers get the golden buzzer or win these competitions.

While this isn't a scientific approach to why certain people stand out and I don't have concrete data, certain themes were repeated over and over during my research. It's become clear that many, if not all, of the following ten elements determine why certain people stand out, even when placed in a group of many other talented and amazing individuals. It's also clear that the more of these you can check off, the more likely you are to stand out for the right person in the right moment. There may be other ways that people stand out, but these are the ones that are the most impactful.

TEN ELEMENTS OF A STANDOUT

1. **Uniqueness**. As I said before, you are unique in your own way and no one can be you (and you can't be anyone else). Your differences make you special. It's hard to stand out if you're the same as everyone else, so you must capitalize on those differences.

2. **Value**. We all want to know "What's in it for me?" People stand out when they provide some sort of utility, importance, or meaning for someone else. This could be a value in the form of entertainment, a good feeling, a monetary reward, or any number of other benefits, but it has to be worth something to the recipient.

3. **Sustainability**. Anyone can be different and stand out once, when everything goes right. The key is to be able to stand out consistently over the long run, even when things aren't going so well, which enhances your brand

image. We desire consistency, and those who stand out repeatedly are the people we remember most.

4. **Likeability**. People must like you and/or have an admiration for you. Companies all over the world have strong, value-added employees with a unique skill who perform consistently well over a long period of time but get passed by for the most visible projects, the best opportunities, and promotions because they're not likeable. That opinion could be from how they treat others or how they go about their job. Maybe something about their smile, clothes, or demeanor doesn't indicate approachability. Sometimes, being the standout who is chosen for something comes down to simply being more likeable than other well-deserving, talented, strong, and capable competitors. Many contestants on *America's Got Talent* or *American Idol* get chosen because they're likeable. We cheer for them and we are inspired by their stories.

5. **Connection**. Working hand in hand with likeability is connection. You might establish a connection with someone who has something you want, or perhaps they've undergone similar experiences. It could also be that you simply feel a positive energy with someone. Connecting with someone means you've separated your personal brand in their minds.

6. **Above Expectations**. As described in *The Power of Moments*, elevation above the norm creates lasting impressions. People stand out when they exceed someone else's expectations, especially if they do so consistently. Even better is that we remember people when they rise above expectations well beyond when they do it.

7. **Extraordinary.** To have the best odds of standing out, you must be extraordinary in your talent, chosen field, skill, relationships, etc. Being extraordinary comes from all the work that you do in private so that you can perform at a high level in public. It's one thing to be different than someone's expectation, but you might be different in the wrong way. To truly stand out, you need to be different and do it in a way that is so extraordinary, we all admire what you can do in the moment. Master your abilities and your craft, and you will master the moments that matter.

8. **Energy.** Have you ever noticed that some people just have a glowing, infectious charisma about them? Energy is constantly moving and transferring around us. You've experienced it before when you've walked into a room and the air is thick with tension, or your mood changed when you ran into someone who was having a bad day. There is actually a term for it called "social contagion," where we tend to take on the energy of a person or group of people we're interacting with. People who have a positive, energetic impact seem to stand out in our hearts and minds. This element is so important that occasionally two people could be equally qualified for a role, a promotion, or even a date, but the one who exudes a more positive energy and vibe will be chosen almost every time.

9. **Sensory Appeal.** These last two standout elements are probably the most important. For starters, you must also have an impact on the senses. This impact could be from sight, sound, smell, or touch, but it could also be a rational and logical appeal (influence). The more senses you can appeal to, the more you'll stand out. As we said before, humans are visual creatures and our eye goes

to that which appeals to it. We also tend to remember things associated with certain smells, sounds, tastes, and we're drawn to the sense of touch. The deeper that your senses are touched, the more you will have an emotional connection.

10. **Emotions.** Most importantly, people rise above the crowd when they move our emotions. Sometimes it's the overwhelming sense of happiness that exudes from their appearance, or it could be touching moments of sadness and empathy from their hearts that moves us. So many times, we want to be associated with and support people who move our emotions in a certain way. As Maya Angelou said, "People will forget what you said. People will forget what you did. But people will never forget how you made them feel." That's why your clothes, the firmness of your handshake, the strength of your resume, and your responses to questions matter on a job interview, but not as much as how you made the interviewer feel about you.

In order to be better than the competition, you need to have as many of the ten elements working in your favor as possible, and you definitely need to have more than others do.

You can also apply these core elements to websites, company brands, people in social media, and other areas. Products, services, experiences, and companies stand out because they rise above the norm, move our emotions, and provide exceptional value for us. They connect deeply to something within us and have some sensory appeal over an extended time period.

What really solidified this list in my mind was when I applied these ten elements to my wife as I was writing this book. I found it so easy to see exactly how she does each one of these for me every day and it helped me understand why I feel the way I do about her. Maybe you can test how they work for you on someone you know, respect, or admire as well.

THE STANDOUT QUADRANTS

As we said before, the ten elements don't come with a guarantee of standing out. Rather, they will help you to create as many opportunities as possible and increase your chance of standing out within those moments.

Standout moments don't happen on their own. You must have two critical elements to increase your chances to stand out when it matters most—differentiation and preparedness. You won't stand out if you're the same as everyone else and you aren't ready for the moment.

To get a better grasp on this key concept, consider a four-quadrant model I call the *Standout Quadrants*. The purpose of this illustration is to represent the critical nature of the intersection between differentiation and preparedness in the moment.

Much of being unique and ready comes down to knowing when those key moments will happen, but it's also highly likely that there will be moments and opportunities to stand out that you didn't know were coming. If you are ready and can leverage your differentiating factor(s), you increase your odds of standing out.

Standout

Opportunity Cost
Spectators
in the Stands

Goals and Dreams
Competitors
in the Arena

LOW
PREPARATION

HIGH
PREPARATION

Wish
Fans at Home

Luck
Players on the
Sidelines

LOW
DIFFERENTIATION

THE GOAL QUADRANT

Your best self and your specific goals reside in the top right portion of the Standout Quadrants model. This is the highest level of preparation and the highest level of differentiation for that particular moment. Success comes from setting goals and having a vision for what will happen, being in a high state of readiness and separating yourself from the field.

This is where standouts play and champions are born. It's called the Goal quadrant, because you're in control, proactively planning, practicing for the moment, and ready to display your talents. You're on the playing field, working hard, and competing for what you want because you're ready and capable. Operating in this area enables you to win because you're in the game, prepared for the moment, and able to capitalize.

Examples of being in the Goal quadrant could be delivering a key presentation in front of senior leaders of your organization, completing a key project on a certain day, getting married, nailing that job interview, or raising an athletic performance in a critical moment of the second half of a playoff game. You live for these moments, know when the moments are happening, and are prepared to crush it when it matters most.

THE LUCK QUADRANT

The bottom-right area of the model is called the Luck quadrant. This is where you might be at your highest level of preparation, but you aren't any different than the rest. Because you're the same as all the other hardworking individuals in this case, you have no control over what happens. A key decision or outcome will be dependent on other differentiating factors. Keeping with the sports analogy, you're on the sidelines when the moment of truth arises.

THE OPPORTUNITY COST QUADRANT

The top left is known as the Opportunity Cost quadrant. Here, you are highly differentiated for one reason or another, but you aren't prepared for the moment, you aren't ready to play, and you lose the opportunity to stand out.

Like being a spectator in the stands, you're in the arena of battle but you aren't prepared to play. You're watching others perform and the cost to you is the lost opportunity.

This will happen most often when you aren't looking ahead, planning, and acting intentionally for the moment. Since you didn't know it would present itself to you, you weren't prepared and ready to capitalize even though you had a differentiating factor to leverage. This is why all that preparation in private, even for the unknown, is so critical to your success in public.

What you do backstage when no one is watching and when you don't know when your chance will come will determine the successes you have when you're onstage. You must be ready when an opportunity comes up, even if you didn't know it was coming.

THE WISH QUADRANT

The last quadrant is the worst of all scenarios. In the Wish Quadrant, you aren't prepared for the situation and you aren't any different from the crowd. You want success and happiness, but you resort to wishing that they happen to you. Year after year passes and those wishes come and go. Resentment and discouragement sets in. You might be enjoying life to some degree, but your dreams and desires never come to fruition. In this game situation, you're a fan at home, watching the game and wishing you could play.

This is the land of the commodity and the area where hard work and determination get lost.

We all occasionally find ourselves in this zone. The good news is that you get to write your story, take control of your life, and do something about it. If your wishes don't come true, you know where to look and who to hold accountable.

By planning ahead, becoming your best, being different than the rest, and preparing for the moment, you can shift your life and career from having wishes to achieving goals.

Interestingly enough, we can layer the previous coffee commodity to experience diagram over the top of the four quadrants. You can see clearly how a commodity (what everyone else does) is in the Wish zone, while the full expressive and amazing experience you provide is in the Goals and Dreams zones.

You can further move towards the upper portion of the top-right box by using your Standout "x-factors" to provide the most differentiation, preparation, and competitive advantage to provide the highest value for someone else (which in turn provides the highest value for you).

THE X-FACTORS

Your ability to prepare for the moment, leverage your uniqueness, and seize the moment, combined with your ability to leverage as many of the standout elements as possible will help you stand out when it matters most.

The acronym STANDOUTX however, ends with an "X," which means there are critical x-factors that bring everything together and comprise your competitive advantage. With these factors, you'll be unstoppable, rise above the competition, and stand out in the hearts, minds, and souls of others.

1. **Experience.** Life is all about experiences, not things. If you can be a positive, emotional, and rewarding experience for others, people will want more of you for their own experience.

2. **Exception.** Being the exception and being different by default helps you to stand out from the crowd. Optimizing your differences to match the needs of the situation will enhance your chances to stand out.

3. **Execution.** You can learn all you want and have the best goals and plans, but it won't matter if you don't execute. Disciplined, focused, and consistent execution wins the war every time. The person who does the most will always beat the person who has the most talent. What good is that talent, idea, or plan if you don't use it?

4. **Expertise.** To stand out, you need to be a master of a craft that others need. You will be hired not only for your potential but also for your expertise.

5. **Excellence.** Your potential and expertise get you part of the way, but how well you do it determines how far you go. You don't have to be perfect, but you must be excellent when it matters most.

6. **Expression.** How you express what you do matters just as much as what you actually do. Modern compensation theory looks at each one with equal weighting.

7. **Excitement.** Emotions mean everything. If you can excite someone with your potential and your performance, you will start to separate from the field.

8. **Exemplify.** It's one thing to know who you are, what leadership is, and how you can make a difference in the world. It's an entirely different thing to exemplify being your greatest self, being an exceptional leader, and being someone who matters. Set the example by showing what's possible for others.

9. **Explore.** Learning, growing, and developing is about exploration. Things don't come to you; you must go to them. The way to do that is to explore, take risks, and try new things. The more you see and do, the more you know.

10. **Exceed.** You must go above and beyond not only what others expect, but what you think you're capable of. Just knowing what others expect of you makes you better than the rest. Delivering above those expectations more consistently than others becomes the standout differentiator. To do this, you must continue to raise your own game to another level. You must exceed the current baseline to see what's possible and achieve what you haven't yet reached.

THE NINE-BOX ASSESSMENT

You won't know if you or someone else stands out without making assessments and getting feedback from others.

Many times, this is a gut feeling (which is why moving emotions is so important). Other times, there are clear KPIs that can be measured against.

A solid way to get an evaluation of how you're doing and evaluate others is to look at this Nine-Box assessment, which compares potential with performance.

Some people have limited potential but are very good at what they do. They're key contributors in an organization but likely won't succeed beyond their current level.

Still others have low potential and their performance is not up to par. They underperform and need coaching. Sometimes, they need to be replaced.

Standouts have high potential and consistently display high

performance. They routinely exceed expectations, which leads others to think that a higher level is always possible. In this way, standouts give people the confidence that they will continue their growth in both areas.

You can use this assessment to determine how you're doing on your path to standing out. Where are you and where do you want to be? Where would you place the people around you?

This assessment works for so many things in your own life. What about your environment, job, and finances?

What about your relationships? The best relationships have the potential to get better and grow, while the everyday performance is consistent and wonderful but not without challenges or tough times. Some relationships are solid but have limited potential, and others lack in both potential and everyday performance.

The key takeaway from using this assessment is to continually evaluate how things are going, leverage what's working, and change what isn't on your way to standing out.

BE THE STANDOUT EXPERIENCE!

In this chapter, you learned why certain people stand out and why others don't. You learned that the key is to combine high levels of preparation with high levels of differentiation. You also learned that the experience of you is a key element to standing out (hence the title of this book).

The standout life does not follow the normal bell curve. As

you go through the years, you get more opportunities to stand out. As you capitalize on those moments, you will feel an increasing presence of The Standout Experience. The more you lead a standout life, radiate a standout experience, and leave a standout impression on the world, the more success and happiness you'll enjoy, and the greater your legacy will be.

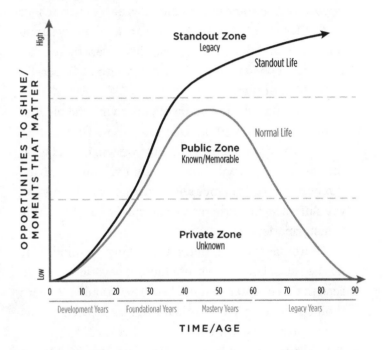

As we close this chapter and come to the end of the playbook, keep in mind this quote from Matshona Dhliwayo...

"Stars don't beg the world for attention; their beauty forces us to look up."

STAIRS TO HELP YOU STAND OUT

Today:

- List three occasions in your past when you stood out. Think about what you did, how you did it, and why you stood out. What can you do again?
- List three occasions in your past where you had the opportunity to stand out but didn't. What could you have done differently? Did you not prepare enough, were you unaware that the opportunity was there, were there other factors that prevented you from standing out? Be careful not to blame others.
- Write on one side of a piece of paper who the old and ordinary you is today and what you do now. On the other side, write who the new standout you will be and what that version of you will do differently. Evaluate your Nine Box current performance and future potential. How can you shift to higher boxes and what will the benefits of this transformation be?
- List ten or more people that stand out in your mind. Why do they stand out? Are there factors beyond what you read in this chapter that made them a standout? Share their stories on social media for others to learn the lessons. You never know who you will inspire.
- Take action and get involved. Join the Standout Movement and start your own journey (www.standout movement.com). Share this with others so they can read the book, join the movement, and work with you on the journey. Establish a chapter in your school, business, or community. Become an ambassador, provide your talents, leverage your expertise, and share your wisdom to help others in the movement.

Every day:

- List two or three key opportunities to stand out today. At the end of the day, reflect on how you demonstrated the Standout Experience.
- What opportunities to stand out will you have tomorrow or in the short term that you can prepare for today? Also, write down your longer-term opportunities to stand out and what one thing you will do to prepare for it.
- In private moments, did you live the Standout Experience when no one was watching? What did you do differently and were you exceptional in those moments? How you do one thing is how you do everything, so these seemingly unimportant moments are actually very important.
- Determine if you were positive, influential, or helpful for someone, and if you demonstrated your standout product, service, or experience today.

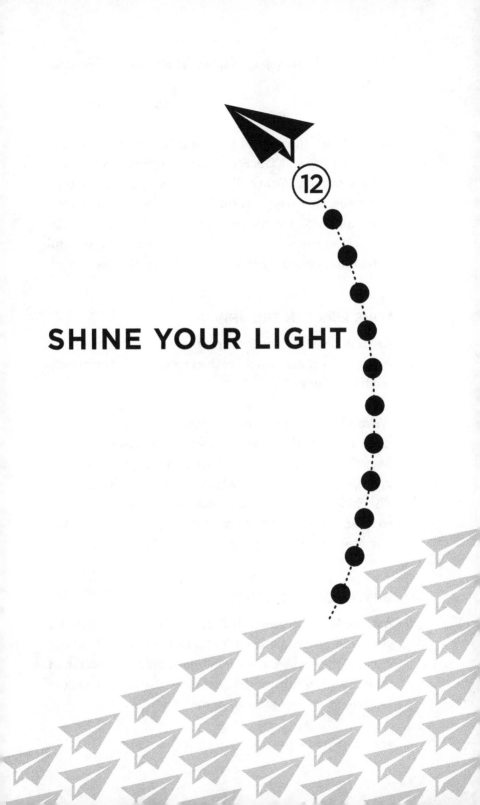

SHINE YOUR LIGHT

"We don't make a living by what we get, we make a life by what we give."

~WINSTON CHURCHILL

As you finish this book, I hope you take away the simple truth that life and The Standout Experience, is only partially about you. We are all but one small pinpoint in time and place. However, even the smallest pebble can have a huge ripple effect on the vast water around it. Likewise, the smallest sun in the vast and dark universe has the powerful potential to create life on planets millions of miles away.

YOUR PLACE IN THE UNIVERSE

As a final piece of advice and inspiration, I'd like you to think of humanity as part of a collective energy that flows throughout the universe.

We're all moving through the cosmos at various speeds and in various directions, but we're all part of something much bigger than ourselves as well. In the vastness of time and space, we are symbolic of what's out there in the universe. The choice is entirely yours about who you want to be, how you want to live, and what impact you want to have on the universe.

DESTRUCTIVE ENTITIES

Asteroids. Some people drift aimlessly through space for years and often collide with others, not caring about the damage they cause. They don't have a clear direction in their life and ultimately live out their existence in endless movement without purpose or meaning.

Black holes. Others are more destructive and spend their life sucking everything into their own existence. Everything is about them. In a black hole, there is no sense of contribution; only a cosmic force that takes anything it can for its own personal gain. There is never enough energy or matter to fill the black hole and they eventually die out with nothing to show for it.

NEUTRAL MASSES

Moons. Some people live within the universe orbiting others but never fully realizing their potential as a life-generating and sustaining planet. They serve a purpose for others, but their pull and gravitational field provides planets with benefits that aren't known or appreciated.

POSITIVE ENTITIES

Shooting stars. These people stand out and they have a brilliance about them, but it's only for a very brief moment. They have fifteen minutes of fame, which takes place like a brilliant flash of light that others admire. Many people see a shooting star and cast their own wishes for a moment of brilliance and light. However, shooting stars vanish into time and space as quickly as they appear for the world to wish upon.

Life-Sustaining Planets. Many people have a warm, friendly core and are capable of sustaining life. They're beautiful and happy in their own way, but they don't necessarily stand out. Their existence depends on the energy of others. These people use that energy for their own beauty to promote and sustain life. While not spectacular, they do serve a specific purpose and are the foundation of life in an otherwise vast and dark universe.

The Sun. This is what you want to aspire to become. People who are like the sun constantly stand out. Their circles of life come together to generate a radiating positive energy from their core. They shine across the darkness of space and give life to others. People want to be around the sun for their light, their warmth, and the energy they provide.

This is your takeaway brain tattoo and your purpose in life. Each day, you have the ability, opportunity, and responsibility to rise and set like the sun, glow from the inside out, shine your beautiful rays of light on others, and leave the world a little better than it was the day before.

As you rise every morning, I want you to think about how you can stand out to make a difference in your own life and everyone else's. As you shine every day, live and be *The Standout Experience* for others.

Don't just remember the words, but continuously take actions that reflect your knowledge, and use your unique gifts and abilities to stand out. As nighttime approaches, think about the ways you positively impacted others and create ways for you to do it all again tomorrow.

The world needs you and all that you have to offer. I hope you find this book to be inspirational and helpful and that you do the work you must do to become the person you are capable of being.

Imagine what you can do and imagine what we can do together as a community of warm and glowing suns that stand out and cast a light for the world...Rise, Shine, and Impact!

APPENDIX A

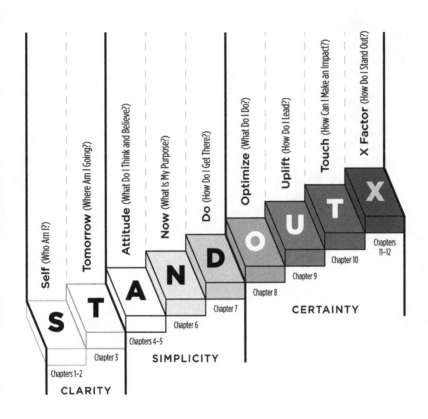

APPENDIX 2

APPENDIX B

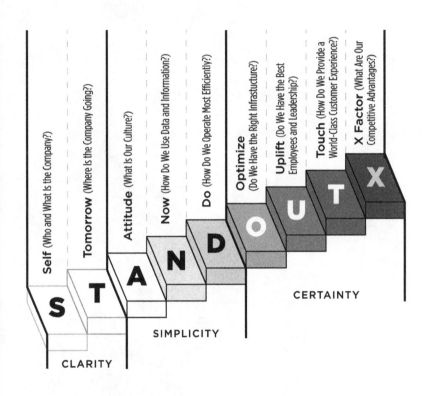

Self (Who and What Is the Company?)

Tomorrow (Where Is the Company Going?)

Attitude (What Is Our Culture?)

Now (How Do We Use Data and Information?)

Do (How Do We Operate Most Efficiently?)

Optimize (Do We Have the Right Infrastucture?)

Uplift (Do We Have the Best Employees and Leadership?)

Touch (How Do We Provide a World-Class Customer Experience?)

X Factor (What Are Our Competitive Advantages?)

CLARITY

SIMPLICITY

CERTAINTY

APPENDIX C

THE STANDOUTX CREED

I write my story. I am in control of my life. I make my own choices, and I own my day. I am the hero character in my life, and I will determine how the story goes. I live my life the way I want to live it, and I'll do whatever it takes to make my story a bestseller.

I am me. I am unique, and I am who I am. I am good with my past, grounded in my present, and moving forward to my future. I grow and develop myself, and I always strive to be my best.

I determine my success. I create my future and determine holistic success on my terms. I follow my North Star with clarity, focus, dedication, grit, and determination. I am willing to experiment and take risks to pursue my *ikigai*. I am motivated and driven to achieve my goals and dreams.

I play the game. I am a champion. I enjoy playing the long game and getting better every day. I embrace challenges, prepare more than others, and have fun. I push myself to the highest level and beyond. I compete hard and never give up.

I am hungry to win, and I love to dominate. I am respectful of others.

I live happy and love deeply. I do what makes me happy, and I have no regrets. I find success in happiness, and I create happiness for others. I do what I love, and I love what I do. I love deeply and unconditionally, and I don't settle for anything less for myself. I always give more than I take.

I live my purpose. I know my purpose, and I rise, shine, and impact every day. I exemplify the power of three and I celebrate leveling up. I value my inputs, optimize my environment, and control my outputs for the benefit of others. I aim to leave a legacy for others.

I take the journey. I know where I'm going, plan ahead, and make good choices. I raise my standards and constantly push myself to be more, do more, and go higher. I rebound from setbacks, and I do what's hard to fight against the gravity of life. I am agile, flexible, and willing to make changes to chart a better course when necessary.

I build my foundations. I lay one brick at a time and set the necessary groundwork for all areas of my life. I execute my plans and take consistent action. I do it even when I don't want to. I work harder than the rest and have the right circles around me. I remain loyal to my daily habits, and I relentlessly prepare myself in all areas of my career and my life.

I take the lead. I set the example, seek knowledge by asking questions, and help raise the potential of those around me. I inspire and help others and show what's possible. I lead change and have a vision for the future. I step up, accept responsibility, and lead for myself and others.

I make an impact. I make a difference and I matter. I solve problems, innovate, create, and add value. I make an impact on the world no matter how big or small. I connect with those around me and positively touch the lives of others.

I stand out. I rise above the norm and stand out when it matters most. I live a standout life and create powerful moments for others. I have high potential and consistently demonstrate high performance. I work hard to be the exception, display excellence, exceed expectations, and exemplify my own personal x-factors.

I shine my light. I live my core values steadily, guard my thoughts and beliefs carefully, and choose my words and actions wisely. I radiate positive energy and shine my light on others.

I am a Standout!

....

SIGNATURE

....

DATE

ABOUT THE AUTHOR

As the President and CEO of StandoutX, LLC and the leader the Standout Movement, **JOHN WALSH** is committed to helping students and young professionals tap into their unlimited potential, create their best life, and make a difference in the world.

John's incredible journey held many challenges, but with a uniquely energetic presence, he overcame them to achieve tremendous personal and professional success.

John is a former senior executive with The Walt Disney Company and The Madison Square Garden Company, but his true passion is as an inspirational speaker and coach to teach young people the importance of standing out. His goal? Reach ten million students in ten years. Will you be one of them?

CPSIA information can be obtained
at www.ICGtesting.com
Printed in the USA
LVHW111153051020
667873LV00042B/81/J